# THE POCKET UNIVERSITY

WALTER SCOTT, BART.

# THE
# POCKET UNIVERSITY
## VOLUME X

# POETRY
## BALLADS OLD AND NEW

EDITED BY
## HENRY VAN DYKE

ASSISTED BY
## HARDIN CRAIG, Ph.D.
AND
## ASA DON DICKINSON

PUBLISHED FOR
# NELSON DOUBLEDAY, INC.

BY
## DOUBLEDAY, PAGE & COMPANY
GARDEN CITY                    NEW YORK
1924

# GENERAL PREFACE

THIS is a collection of *Little Masterpieces of Poetry*. The title of the collection gives the clue to the principle of choice. This is not an attempt to make another historical anthology of English verse, giving illustrations of the work of every acknowledged poet more or less famous, and carefully apportioning the number of selections from each writer according to the supposed measure of his fame. That question, indeed, has not entered into the process of choice, to disturb and hamper it. It has not been necessary to ask whether too much has been taken from one poet, or too little from another. I have looked only at the value and the beauty of the poems themselves, at their perfection as poetry, at the clearness, strength, and depth of their feeling, at the truth and vividness of their imagery, at the power or the loveliness of their expression and form. Those that seemed the best have been chosen out of many, not to illustrate a theory, but for their own sake, because they are good to read.

A masterpiece, of course, cannot be a fragment or an extract. It must stand alone, complete and rounded; and no matter how small it may be, it must carry within itself its own claim to excellence. For this reason I have not included any disconnected portions of longer poems, or brilliant passages from works which as a whole are not of even merit. Each poem that has been chosen is given in its entirety, as the author wrote it. The only exception is in the case of certain songs and lyrics, which can be taken out of their setting in a play or a story, without marring either their form or their effect; and this is not an exception in reality, but only in appearance.

Some poems of great beauty, like Milton's *Comus* and Tennyson's *Maud*, reluctant as I am to omit them, are ruled out by the limitation of space. The same reason explains the fact that dramas are omitted, and that the epic element also is lacking, except in its minor forms, the idyll and the story in verse, and in its lyrical modification, the ballad.

I have thought it wise, also, not to include any metrical translations of poetry from other languages; for, however admirable they may be as renderings of the originals, they can hardly rank as English masterpieces. To deserve that title a poem must be conceived and composed, as well as written, in the English language. It makes no difference where the poet was born, in Scotland or England or Ireland or America, if his poetry came to him in English, it belongs to English literature, the common heritage of all the races and tribes which use that noble language as their own.

In the gathering and the sifting of the materials for this collection my colleague, Dr. Hardin

# General Preface

Craig, has rendered much valuable assistance, which is here gratefully acknowledged. The selection of the particular text of the poems, the reading of proofs, and the insertion of dates have been entrusted to his scholarly care.

The poems have been grouped on a principle of arrangement which seems to me both new and good—the principle of poetic form. Thus in one part we have ballads, in another idylls and stories in verse, in another lyrics, in another odes, sonnets and epigrams, in another elegies and epitaphs. This method of grouping not only brings together the poems which are most alike in their effect (a matter of the first importance to the reader's comfort and pleasure), but also serves to show how significant and how vital the element of form is in poetry. It is not a mere accident or an unimportant adjunct. The spirit and the body are the man; the substance and the form are the poem. There is usually more kinship, for example, between two ballads dealing with different subjects, like *Thomas the Rhymer* and Longfellow's *Sir Humphrey Gilbert*, than there is between a ballad and a sonnet dealing with the same subject, like Coleridge's *Love* and one of Mrs. Browning's *Sonnets from the Portuguese*.

This arrangement by poetic form has also another advantage, which I have had in view in anticipating a possible use of this volume in colleges and schools and by private students. It will enable the reader to follow, without effort, the development of the various forms of verse, and to see how a ballad or a lyric or a sonnet of the sixteenth century differs from one of the nineteenth. As far as possible, the date of the publication of each poem has been printed with the author's name. When the date of composition is widely different from that of publication it has also been added; such dates are printed in italics.

Within the main divisions, the poems have been grouped in a rather loose way, according to their subjects; and within these minor groups again, a chronological order has been generally followed. Thus it will be found, unless I am mistaken, that one can read on from poem to poem without serious discord, and with a certain continuity of interest and feeling.

The amount of verse taken from the British poets is, of course, much greater than that which comes from the American poets. The reason is plain. In the former case there are four centuries of poetry to choose from, and in the latter case less than a hundred years. But unless this altogether fails in its purpose, one result of reading it will be a clearer understanding and a deeper sense of the vital relationship of that which is best, that which is permanent, in British and in American verse. They are not separate growths. They are the two main branches of a great and spreading tree. The elder branch is far larger, and has borne far more fruit, than the younger. But the difference is one of degree and not of kind; and the years to come may lessen even that.

Meantime it is certain that the loftiest thoughts

and imaginings, the deepest and noblest feelings, the finest hopes, and the fairest dreams of all

> "Who speak the tongue
> That Shakespeare spake; the faith and morals hold
> Which Milton held,"

are embodied in the masterpieces of English poetry, of which a goodly number are brought together in this volume. Put this on your shelves, and you will not lack good comradeship, and elevating discourse, and music by the way.

HENRY VAN DYKE.

## NOTE FOR THE NEW EDITION

This brief series of "little masterpieces" in verse has found so warm a welcome and has been so often reprinted, that the original plan on which it was made seems to stand the test of use, and a new edition is demanded. There has been no alteration in the general scheme of the anthology, which was quite novel when it was first put forth in 1905. The poems are chosen not for academic reasons but for the poetic pleasure which they impart to a healthy mind. They are grouped in a way that follows natural affinity and makes it easier for the reader to wander on from one to another. In harmony with these ideas the collection has now been enlarged, and I hope enriched, by additions from the later poetry. (I will not call it "the *new* poetry," because the phrase is meaningless; all good poems, however ancient their date, have an everlasting newness in them which custom cannot stale.)

# General Preface

The responsibility and credit for making these selections belong to my colleague, Mr. Asa Don Dickinson, Librarian of the University of Pennsylvania, to whose skilful and experienced hand this task has been committed, and whose name I am thus privileged to put upon the title-page as one of the editors. His choice carries my full consent. I could only wish that he had found more modern poems to bring into the fold of beauty

"Which bards in fealty to Apollo hold."

October 8, 1921.

H. v. D.

# CONTENTS

# Contents

# Contents

# Contents

# ACKNOWLEDGMENT

THE texts used in these volumes follow closely what were thought to be the best available modern editions; except that punctuation has been, now and then, in cases where no change of meaning would arise, made to conform to a more general standard. The dating of the poems has been done from the work of editors and biographers, as in a vast majority of cases original editions have not been at hand. In the case of a few poems the date is that of earliest publication in book form. Sometimes the composition date has been thought more significant, or found more convenient.

The selections included in these volumes from Ralph Waldo Emerson, Oliver Wendell Holmes, Bret Harte, Lucy Larcom, James Russell Lowell, H. W. Longfellow, Thomas William Parsons, Bayard Taylor, J. G. Whittier, E. R. Sill, and Celia Thaxter are published by permission of, and by special arrangement with, Houghton, Mifflin & Co., authorized publishers of the works of those authors. The selections from the poems of William Morris are reprinted by permission of

# Acknowledgment

Longmans, Green & Co. The two poems by Paul Hamilton Hayne are copyrighted, 1882, by D. Lothrop & Co. "Anthony and Cleopatra" by Gen. Wm. H. Lytle is published by permission of Robert Clarke Co., the publishers of his poems. The two poems by Emily Dickinson are reprinted by permission of Little, Brown & Co. Charles Scribner's Sons, as authorized publishers, have granted permission for the republication of "Little Boy Blue," "Wynken, Blynken, and Nod" from "With Trumpet and Drum" by Eugene Field; of "A Ballad of Trees and the Master," "The Stirrup Cup," "Sunrise," "The Marshes of Glynn" from "The Poems of Sidney Lanier"; of "It Never Comes Again," "The Sky" from "The Poetical Writings of Richard Henry Stoddard"; and of "Requiem," "The Whaups," "Youth and Love" from "Poems and Ballads" by Robert Louis Stevenson. The selections from Matthew Arnold are from the edition issued by The Macmillan Company, the authorized publishers of the works of Matthew Arnold.

H. C.

The "Selections from the Later Poetry" are all protected by copyright and are reprinted here by arrangement with the authors or their publishers, to whom the editor extends his grateful acknowledgments.

A. D. D.

BALLADS OLD AND NEW

# INTRODUCTION
# TO THE VOLUME OF BALLADS

WHAT is a ballad?

In the strict sense of the word, it ought to mean a song set to dance music,—a string of verses to accompany the movements of a rustic or courtly *ballet*. But this original meaning was soon lost and confused in a wider usage. The word was applied to many kinds of poems which were current among the people in the fifteenth and the sixteenth centuries. Metrical tales of love and adventure and tragedy, versified satires on the nobility and the clergy, moral exhortations and short sermons in rhyme, lyrics in praise of a sweetheart or a soldier,—almost any piece of poetry that passed from mouth to mouth among the minstrels, or was printed on broadside sheets and sold by the pedlars, who were the book-canvassers of that day,—might be called a "tragical ballett," or a "godly ballett," or a "diverting ballett," according to the supposed effect upon the hearer. The chaplain of Henry VIII quoted in one of his sermons, "the ballates off 'Passe tyme with goodde cumpanye' and 'I love unlovydde.'" In the Bishops' Bible the title of Solomon's Song is "The Ballet of the Ballets of Solomon."

3

No distinction was made, in those early times, between narrative ballads and other songs; nor between those which had their anonymous origin among the people and those which were carefully wrought out by certain poets. Indeed, the term "ballade," so far as it had a technical sense, was used to describe one of the most artificial and difficult forms of verse, which could be written only by a skilled master.

The attempt to restrict the use of the name "ballad" to story-poems which are traditional in character and purely popular in origin and form, is a somewhat modern invention. Famous collections of such poems have been made; Percy's *Reliques of Ancient English Poetry,* Ritson's *Robin Hood,* Scott's *Minstrelsy of the Scottish Border,* Motherwell's *Minstrelsy Ancient and Modern,* Child's *English and Scottish Popular Ballads,* and many other books of the same kind, are filled with the naïve, irregular, graphic, and often strangely beautiful narratives in rhyme which have been handed down to us without an author's name, preserved and transmitted by the loving memory of the people. And these, some critics say, are the only true ballads, because they are not the work of personal poets, but the unconscious flowerings of poetry from the common heart of man. It seems to me that this effort to narrow the meaning of the word is misdirected, and that the reason which the critics give for it begs the whole question.

The fact that no author's name is attached to

4

the rude and vigorous verses of *A Gest of Robyn Hode,* or *The Battle of Otterbourne,* does not prove that they never had an author, but only that he has been forgotten. Verses do not come to the birth without the aid of some minstrel to give them form and set them to music. A community never makes a poem. It is a man who makes it. The community, if the age is poetical, takes the song-story up, and repeats it, in hall and cottage, with changes and variations. So it comes to us, from a time when books were rare and copyright was unknown, in half a dozen different forms, and often with great improvements, but without the name of the original minstrel. This, it seems to me, is the true explanation of what is called "communal authorship,"—an unseen poet singing in obscurity,—his song caught up and carried down to us by the love of the people. Coleridge was instinctively right when he wrote of

> "the *bard* . . . who made
> The grand old ballad of Sir Patrick Spence."

Moreover, even if we accepted at its face value the notion that the primitive ballads were made by a whole village, or a county perhaps, or even an entire kingdom, rhyming in unconscious unison, why should we be more narrow and particular in our definition of ballads than the very people who made them? They were willing to admit that King James's *The Kingis Quair* and Lord Dorset's *"To all you ladies"* were ballads.

It is hardly likely that the critics will be able to confine the use of the word "ballad" to the limited sense which some of them have assigned to it. Language has a way of escaping from the control of the learned and making its own connections with human life. There are folk-words as well as folk-songs. And this very word "ballad" which we are considering is one of them. It has followed its own course in common speech and writing. It is no longer applied, it is true, to purely lyrical songs, or to hymns, or to didactic verse. But it is still used to describe poems, differing considerably in form and origin, which have three main characteristics in common.

First, they have a certain simplicity of theme, appealing not to reflection or to philosophic thought (as an epic or an idyll does), but more directly to some strong, common, human feeling of wonder, of admiration, or of pity. Second, they have an interesting story, clear and vivid, either told directly (as in *The Bailiff's Daughter*), or suggested in the background (as in *Fair Helen*). Third, they are free and lyrical in spirit and movement, not composed in blank-verse, or in complicated stanzas, but in more flowing and easy forms. These are the three characteristics that have been followed in selecting the ballads in this volume.

I do not suppose that all the good ones are here: but I think that all here are good. Some of them, perhaps, come very near to the border-line of the story in verse, or of the pure lyric:

# Introduction

just as some of the poems in the second and third
volumes of this series might possibly be called
ballads and included here. The affair of classify-
ing poetry is not like a chemical analysis or a
land survey. There is always room for a difference, and sometimes for a change, of opinion.

But, upon the whole, I am satisfied that these
poems represent the mastery of the ballad-form
and illustrate its history. Ranging from *The
Death of Robin Hood* to *Rizpah,* from *Young
Beichan* to *Amy Wentworth,* from *Sir Patrick
Spens* to *The Wreck of the Schooner Hesperus,*
they give a rich and splendid picture of the ballad-
poetry of love, of fairyland, of adventure, of the
sea, of war, and of death and sorrow.

H. v. D.

OF LOVE

# THE GAY GOSHAWK

"O WALY, waly, my gay goshawk,
    Gin your feathering be sheen!"
"And waly, waly, my master dear,
    Gin ye look pale and lean!

"O have ye tint at tournament    5
    Your sword, or yet your spear?
Or mourn ye for the Southern lass,
    Whom ye may not win near?"

"I have not tint, at tournament,
    My sword, nor yet my spear;    10
But sair I mourn for my true-love,
    Wi' mony a bitter tear.

"But weel 's me on ye, my gay goshawk,
    Ye can baith speak and flee;
Ye sall carry a letter to my love,    15
    Bring an answer back to me."

"But how sall I your true-love find,
    Or how suld I her know?
I bear a tongue ne'er wi' her spake,
    An eye that ne'er her saw."    20

11

"O weel sall ye my true-love ken,
   Sae sune as ye her see;
For of a' the flowers of fair England,
   The fairest flower is she.

"The red that's on my true-love's cheek, 25
   Is like blood-drops on the snaw;
The white, that is on her breast bare,
   Like the down o' the white sea-maw.

"And even at my love's bour-door
   There grows a flowering birk; 30
And ye maun sit and sing thereon,
   As she gangs to the kirk.

"And four-and-twenty fair ladies
   Will to the mass repair;
But weel may ye my lady ken, 35
   The fairest lady there."

Lord William has written a love-letter,
   Put it under his pinion gray;
And he is awa' to Southern land,
   As fast as wings can gae. 40

And even at that lady's bour,
   There grew a flowering birk;
And he sat down and sung thereon,
   As she gaed to the kirk.

And weel he kent that lady fair 45
   Amang her maidens free,

# The Gay Goshawk

For the flower that springs in May morning
    Was not sae sweet as she.

And first he sang a low, low note,
    And syne he sang a clear;    50
And aye the o'erword o' the sang
    Was, " Your love can no win here."

" Feast on, feast on, my maidens a',
    The wine flows you amang,
While I gang to my shot-window,    55
    And hear yon bonny bird's sang.

" Sing on, sing on, my bonny bird,
    The sang ye sung yestreen;
For weel I ken, by your sweet singing,
    Ye are frae my true-love sen'."    60

O first he sang a merry sang,
    And syne he sang a grave;
And syne he peck'd his feathers gray,
    To her the letter gave.

" Have there a letter from Lord William;    65
    He says he 's sent ye three;
He canna wait your love langer,
    But for your sake he 'll die."

" Gae bid him bake his bridal bread,
    And brew his bridal ale;    70
And I sall meet him at Mary's kirk,
    Lang, lang ere it be stale."

The lady's gane to her chamber,
  And a moanfu' woman was she,
As gin she had ta'en a sudden brash,   75
  And were about to die.


"A boon, a boon, my father dear,
  A boon I beg of thee!"
"Ask not that paughty Scottish lord,
  For him you ne'er shall see.   80


"But, for your honest asking else,
  Weel granted it shall be."
"Then, gin I die in Southern land,
  In Scotland gar bury me.


"And the first kirk that ye come to,   85
  Ye'se gar the mass be sung;
And the next kirk that ye come to,
  Ye'se gar the bells be rung;


"And when ye come to St. Mary's kirk,
  Ye'se tarry there till night."   90
And so her father pledged his word,
  And so his promise plight.


She has ta'en her to her bigly bour,
  As fast as she could fare,
And she has drank a sleepy draught,   95
  That she had mix'd wi' care.


And pale, pale grew her rosy cheek,
  That was sae bright of blee;

14

# The Gay Goshawk

And she seemed to be as surely dead
    As any one could be.       100


They drapt a drap o' the burning red gowd,
    They drapt it on her chin;
"And ever alas!" her mother cried,
    "There is nae life within."


They drapt a drap o' the burning red
    gowd,       105
    They drapt it on her breast-bane;
"Alas!" her seven bauld brothers said,
    "Our sister's dead and gane."


Then up arose her seven brethren,
    And hew'd to her a bier;       110
They hew'd it frae the solid aik,
    Laid it o'er wi' silver clear.


Then up and gat her seven sisters,
    And sewed to her a kell;
And every steek that they pat in,       115
    Sewed to a siller bell.


The first Scots kirk that they cam to,
    They gar'd the bells be rung;
The next Scots kirk that they cam to,
    They gar'd the mass be sung.       120


But when they cam to St. Mary's kirk,
    There stude spearmen all on raw;

And up and started Lord William,
    The chieftain amang them a'.

"Set down, set down the bier," he said; 125
    "Let me look her upon."
But as soon as Lord William touched her
    hand,
    Her colour began to come.

She brightened like the lily-flower,
    Till her pale colour was gone;   130
With rosy cheek, and ruby lip,
    She smiled her love upon.

"A morsel of your bread, my lord,
    And one glass of your wine;
For I ha'e fasted these three lang days,  135
    All for your sake and mine.

"Gae hame, gae hame, my seven bauld
    brothers,
    Gae hame and blaw your horn!
I trow you wad ha'e gi'en me the skaith,
    But I 've gi'en you the scorn."   140

"Ah! woe to you, you light woman;
    An ill death may you die!
For we left father and mother at hame,
    Breaking their hearts for thee."

                *Scott, Minst. Scot. Bord.*

# YOUNG BEICHAN

In London city was Beichan born,
  He long'd strange countries for to see,
But he was ta'en by a savage Moor,
  Who handl'd him right cruelly.          4

For thro' his shoulder he put a bore,
  An' thro' the bore has pitten a tree,
An' he's gar'd him draw the carts o' wine,
  Where horse and oxen had wont to be.    8

He's casten him in a dungeon deep,
  Where he cou'd neither hear nor see;
He's shut him up in a prison strong,
  An' he's handl'd him right cruelly.     12

The savage Moor had but ae dochter,
  And her name it was Susie Pye,
And ilka day as she took the air,
  The prison door she passèd bye.         16

But it fell ance upon a day,
  As she was walking, she heard him sing;
She listen'd to his tale of woe,
  A happy day for young Beichan!          20

17

"My hounds they all go masterless,
    My hawks they flee frae tree to tree,
My youngest brother will heir my lands,
    My native land I'll never see."    24

"O were I but the prison-keeper,
    As I'm a ladie o' hie degree,
I soon wad set this youth at large,
    And send him to his ain country."    28

She went away into her chamber,
    All nicht she never closed her ee;
And when the morning begoud to dawn,
    At the prison door alane was she.    32

"O hae ye ony lands or rents,
    Or cities in your ain country,
Cou'd free you out of prison strong,
    An' cou'd maintain a lady free?"    36

"O London city is my own,
    An' other cities twa or three,
Cou'd loose me out o' prison strong,
    An' cou'd maintain a lady free."    40

O she has bribed her father's men
    Wi' meikle goud and white money,
She's gotten the key o' the prison doors,
    And she has set young Beichan free.    44

She's gi'n him a loaf o' good white bread,
    But an' a flask o' Spanish wine,

An' she bad' him mind on the lady's love
    That sae kindly freed him out o' pine.   48

"Go set your foot on good ship-board,
    An' haste you back to your ain country,
An' before that seven years has an end,
    Come back again, love, and marry me."   52

It was long or seven years had an end;
    She long'd fu' sair her love to see;
She 's set her foot on good ship-board,
    An' turn'd her back on her ain country.   56

She 's sail'd up, so has she doun,
    Till she came to the other side;
She 's landed at young Beichan's gates,
    An' I hope this day she sall be his bride.   60

"Is this young Beichan's gates?" says she,
    "Or is that noble prince within?"
"He 's up the stairs wi' his bonny bride,
    An' mony a lord and lady wi' him."   64

"O has he ta'en a bonny bride,
    An' has he clean forgotten me!"
An' sighing said that gay lady,
    "I wish I were in my ain country."   68

But she 's pitten her han' in her pocket,
    An' gi'n the porter guineas three;
Says, "Take ye that, ye proud porter,
    An' bid the bridegroom speak to me."   72

O whan the porter came up the stair,
   He's fa'n low down upon his knee;
"Won up, won up, ye proud porter,
   An' what makes a' this courtesy?"      76

"O I've been porter at your gates
   This mair nor seven years an' three,
But there is a lady at them now
   The like of whom I never did see.      80

"For on every finger she has a ring,
   An' on the mid-finger she has three,
An' there's as meikle goud aboon her brow
   As would but an earldome o' lan' to me."  84

Then up it started young Beichan,
   An' sware so loud by our Lady,
"It can be nane but Susie Pye,
   That has come o'er the sea to me."      88

O quickly ran he down the stair,
   O' fifteen steps he has made but three;
He's tane his bonny love in his arms,
   An' a wot he kiss'd her tenderly.      92

"O hae you tane a bonny bride?
   An' hae you quite forsaken me?
An' hae ye quite forgotten her
   That gae you life and liberty?"      96

She's lookit o'er her left shoulder
   To hide the tears stood in her ee;

## The Bonny Earl of Murray

"Now fare thee well, young Beichan," she says,
  "I'll strive to think nae mair on thee."  100

"Take back your daughter, madam," he says,
  "An' a double dowry I'll gi' her wi';
For I maun marry my first true love,
  That's done and suffered so much for
    me."  104

He's take his bonny love by the han',
  An' led her to yon fountain stane;
He's changed her name frae Susie Pye,
  An' he's call'd her his bonny love, Lady
    Jane.  108

*Child, Pop. Bal., No. 53A (Gummere's Version).*


## THE BONNY EARL OF MURRAY

Ye Highlands and ye Lawlands,
  O where hae ye been?
They hae slain the Earl of Murray,
  And they laid him on the green.

Now wae be to thee, Huntley!  5
  And wherefore did ye sae?
I bade you bring him wi' you,
  But forbade you him to slay.

21

He was a braw gallant,
　And he rid at the ring;　　　　10
And the bonny Earl of Murray,
　Oh he might have been a king!

He was a braw gallant,
　And he play'd at the ba';
And the bonny Earl of Murray　　15
　Was the flower amang them a'!

He was a braw gallant,
　And he play'd at the glove;
And the bonny Earl of Murray,
　Oh he was the Queen's love!　　20

Oh lang will his Lady
　Look o'er the Castle Down,
Ere she see the Earl of Murray
　Come sounding thro' the town!

*Child, Pop. Bal., No. 181A.*

# THE BAILIFF'S DAUGHTER OF ISLINGTON

There was a youth, and a well-beloved youth,
　And he was a squire's son:
He loved the bailiff's daughter dear,
　That lived in Islington.

22

# The Bailiff's Daughter of Islington

Yet she was coy and would not believe          5
   That he did love her so,
No, nor at any time would she
   Any countenance to him show.

But when his friends did understand
   His fond and foolish mind,          10
They sent him up to fair London
   An apprentice for to bind.

And when he had been seven long years,
   And never his love could see:
"Many a tear have I shed for her sake,          15
   When she little thought of me."

Then all the maids of Islington
   Went forth to sport and play,
All but the bailiff's daughter dear;
   She secretly stole away.          20

She pulled off her gown of green,
   And put on ragged attire,
And to fair London she would go
   Her true love to enquire.

And as she went along the high road,          25
   The weather being hot and dry,
She sat her down upon a green bank,
   And her true love came riding by.

She started up, with a color so red,
   Catching hold of his bridle-rein;          30

23

"One penny, one penny, kind sir," she said,
  "Will ease me of much pain."

"Before I give you one penny, sweetheart,
    Pray tell me where you were born."
"At Islington, kind sir," said she,       35
  "Where I have had many a scorn."

"I prithee, sweetheart, then tell to me,
    O tell me, whether you know
The bailiff's daughter of Islington."
  "She is dead, sir, long ago."      40

"If she be dead, then take my horse,
    My saddle and bridle also;
For I will into some far country,
    Where no man shall me know."

"O stay, O stay, thou goodly youth,    45
    She standeth by thy side;
She is here alive, she is not dead,
    And ready to be thy bride."

"O farewell grief, and welcome joy,
    Ten thousand times therefore;    50
For now I have found mine own true love,
    Whom I thought I should never see more."

*Percy, Reliques.*

# HIND HORN

"HIND HORN fair, and Hind Horn free,
  O where were you born, in what countrie?"

"In gude green-wood, there I was born,
  And all my forebears me beforn.

"O seven years I served the king,         5
  And as for wages, I never gat nane;

"But ae sight o' his ae daughter,
  And that was thro' an auger-bore.

"My love ga'e me a siller wand,
  'T was to rule over a' Scotland.      10

"And she ga'e me a gay gowd ring,
  The virtue o' 't was above a' thing.

"'As lang 's this ring it keeps the hue,
  Ye 'll know I am a lover true:

"'But when the ring turns pale and wan,   15
  Ye 'll know I love another man.'"

He hoist up sails, and awa' sail'd he,
  And sail'd into a far countrie.

And when he look'd upon his ring,
He knew she loved another man.                    20

He hoist up sails and home came he,
Home unto his ain countrie.

The first he met on his own land,
It chanc'd to be a beggar man.

"What news, what news, my gude auld man?    25
What news, what news ha'e ye to me?"

"Nae news, nae news," said the auld man,
"The morn's our queen's wedding day."

"Will ye lend me your begging weed?
And I'll lend you my riding steed."               30

"My begging weed will ill suit thee,
And your riding steed will ill suit me."

But part be right, and part be wrang,
Frae the beggar man the cloak he wan.

"Auld man, come tell to me your leed;            35
What news ye gi'e when ye beg your bread."

"As ye walk up unto the hill,
Your pike staff ye lend ye till.

"But whan ye come near by the yett,
Straight to them ye will upstep.                   40

# Hind Horn

"Take nane frae Peter, nor frae Paul,
Nane frae high or low o' them all.

"And frae them all ye will take nane,
Until it comes frae the bride's ain hand."

He took nane frae Peter nor frae Paul,    45
Nane frae the high nor low o' them all.

And frae them all he would take nane,
Until it came frae the bride's ain hand.

The bride came tripping down the stair,
The combs o' red gowd in her hair.    50

A cup o' red wine in her hand,
And that she ga'e to the beggar man.

Out o' the cup he drank the wine,
And into the cup he dropt the ring.

"O got ye 't by sea, or got ye 't by land,    55
Or got ye 't on a drown'd man's hand?"

"I got it not by sea, nor got it by land,
Nor got I it on a drown'd man's hand.

"But I got it at my wooing gay,
And I 'll gi'e 't you on your wedding day."    60

"I 'll take the red gowd frae my head,
And follow you, and beg my bread.

'I 'll take the red gowd frae my hair,
And follow you for evermair."

Atween the kitchen and the ha',                  65
He loot his cloutie cloak down fa',

And wi' red gowd shone ower them a',
And frae the bridegroom the bride he sta'.

*Child, Pop. Bal., No. 17H.*


# WALY, WALY, UP THE BANK

### [JAMIE DOUGLAS]

O WALY, waly, up the bank,
  And waly, waly, doun the brae,
And waly, waly, yon burn-side,
  Where I and my love wont to gae!      4

I lean'd my back unto an aik,
  I thocht it was a trustie tree;
But first it bow'd and syne it brak—
  Sae my true love did lichtlie me.      8

O waly, waly, gin love be bonnie
  A little time while it is new!
But when 't is auld it waxeth cauld,
  And fades awa' like morning dew.      12

# Waly, Waly, Up the Bank

O wherefore should I busk my heid,
   Or wherefore should I kame my hair?
For my true love has me forsook,
   And says he 'll never lo'e me mair.    16


Now Arthur's Seat sall be my bed,
   The sheets sall ne'er be 'filed by me;
Saint Anton's well sall be my drink;
   Since my true love has forsaken me.    20


Marti'mas wind, when wilt thou blaw,
   And shake the green leaves aff the tree?
O gentle Death, when wilt thou come?
   For of my life I am wearie.    24


'T is not the frost that freezes fell,
   Nor blawing snaw's inclemencie;
'T is not sic cauld that makes me cry,
   But my love's heart grown cauld to me.    28


When we cam in by Glasgow toun,
   We were a comely sicht to see;
My love was clad in the black velvet,
   And I mysel' in cramasie.    32


But had I wist, before I kist,
   That love had been sae ill to win,
I 'd lock'd my heart in a case o' gowd,
   And pinn'd it wi' a siller pin.    36

>     And O! if my young babe were born,
>       And set upon the nurse's knee;
>     And I mysel' were dead and gane,
>       For a maid again I 'll never be.        40

*Child, Pop. Bal., No. 204a*

## AULD ROBIN GRAY

> WHEN the sheep are in the fauld, and the kye 's
>       come hame,
> And a' the warld to rest are gané,
> The waes o' my heart fa' in showers frae my e'e,
> Unkent by my gudeman, wha sleeps sound by
>       me.                                    4

> Young Jamie lo'ed me weel, and sought me for
>       his bride;
> But saving ae croun-piece he had naething else
>       beside:
> To make the croun a pund, young Jamie gaed to
>       sea;
> And the croun and the pund—they were baith
>       for me.                                8

> He hadna been awa' a week but only twa,
> When my father brak his arm, and the cow was
>       stown awa';
> My mother she fell sick—and my Jamie at the
>       sea—
> And auld Robin Gray came a-courting me.      12

30

# Auld Robin Gray

My father couldna work, and my mother couldna
    spin;
I toil'd day and night, but their bread I couldna
    win;
Auld Rob maintain'd them baith, and wi' tears in
    his e'e
Said, "Jennie, for their sakes, will ye no marry
    me?"

My heart it said nay; I look'd for Jamie back;
But the wind it blew high, and the ship it was a
    wrack;
His ship it was a wrack—Why didna Jamie dee?
Or why am I spared to cry, Wae 's me!    20

My father urged me sair: my mother didna speak;
But she look'd in my face till my heart was like
    to break:
They gi'ed him my hand, tho' my heart was in
    the sea;
Sae auld Robin Gray he was gudeman to me.    24

I hadna been a wife a week but only four,
When mournfu' as I sat on the stane at my door,
I saw my Jamie's wraith,—for I couldna think
    it he,
Till he said, "I 'm come hame, love, to marry
    thee."    28

O sair, sair did we greet, and muckle say of a';
I gi'ed him but ae kiss, and bade him gang awa':

I wish that I were dead, but I 'm no like to dee;
For, though my heart is broken, I 'm but young,
    wae 's me!               32

I gang like a ghaist, and I carena much to spin;
I daurna think on Jamie, for that wad be a sin;
But I 'll do my best a gude wife aye to be,
For auld Robin Gray he is kind to me.     36

   *1771.*                     *Lady Anne Lindsay.*


## BLACK-EYED SUSAN

ALL in the Downs the fleet was moored,
  The streamers waving in the wind,
When black-eyed Susan came aboard;
  " O, where shall I my true-love find?
Tell me, ye jovial sailors, tell me true,
If my sweet William sails among the crew."  6

William, who high upon the yard
  Rocked with the billow to and fro,
Soon as her well-known voice he heard,
  He sighed, and cast his eyes below:
The cord slides swiftly through his glowing
    hands,
And quick as lightning on the deck he
    stands.              12

# Black-eyed Susan

So the sweet lark, high poised in air,
  Shuts close his pinions to his breast,
If chance his mate's shrill call he hear,
  And drops at once into her nest:—
The noblest captain in the British fleet
Might envy William's lip those kisses sweet. 18

"O Susan, Susan, lovely dear,
  My vows shall ever true remain;
Let me kiss off that falling tear;
  We only part to meet again.
Change as ye list, ye winds; my heart shall be
The faithful compass that still points to thee. 24

"Believe not what the landmen say
  Who tempt with doubts thy constant mind:
They'll tell thee, sailors, when away,
  In every port a mistress find:
Yes, yes, believe them when they tell thee so,
For thou art present wheresoe'er I go.    30

"If to fair India's coast we sail,
  Thy eyes are seen in diamonds bright,
Thy breath is Afric's spicy gale,
  Thy skin is ivory so white.
Thus every beauteous object that I view
Wakes in my soul some charm of lovely
    Sue.                    36

"Though battle call me from thy arms,
  Let not my pretty Susan mourn;
Though cannons roar, yet safe from harms
  William shall to his dear return.

Love turns aside the balls that round me fly,
Lest precious tears should drop from Susan's
eye."        42

The boatswain gave the dreadful word,
   The sails their swelling bosom spread;
No longer must she stay aboard:
   They kissed, she sighed, he hung his head.
Her lessening boat unwilling rows to land;
"Adieu!" she cried; and waved her lily hand. 48

1720.                                          *John Gay.*

## THE SAILOR'S WIFE

AND are ye sure the news is true?
   And are ye sure he's weel?
Is this a time to think o' wark?
   Ye jades, lay by your wheel;
Is this the time to spin a thread,
   When Colin's at the door?
Reach down my cloak, I'll to the quay,
   And see him come ashore.
For there's nae luck about the house,
   There's nae luck at a';
There's little pleasure in the house
   When our gudeman's awa'.        12

And gie to me my bigonet,
   My bishop's-satin gown;
For I maun tell the baillie's wife
   That Colin's in the town.

# The Sailor's Wife

My Turkey slippers maun gae on,
  My stockin's pearly blue;
It 's a' to pleasure our gudeman,
  For he 's baith leal and true.          20


Rise, lass, and mak a clean fireside,
  Put on the muckle pot;
Gie little Kate her button gown,
  And Jock his Sunday coat;
And mak their shoon as black as slaes,
  Their hose as white as snaw;
It 's a' to please my ain gudeman,
  For he 's been long awa'.               28


There 's twa fat hens upo' the coop
  Been fed this month and mair;
Mak haste and thraw their necks about,
  That Colin weel may fare;
And spread the table neat and clean,
  Gar ilka thing look braw,
For wha can tell how Colin fared
  When he was far awa'?                   36


Sae true his heart, sae smooth his speech,
  His breath like caller air;
His very foot has music in 't
  As he comes up the stair,—
And will I see his face again?
  And will I hear him speak?
I 'm downright dizzy wi' the thought,
  In troth I 'm like to greet!           44

If Colin 's weel, and weel content,
 I hae nae mair to crave:
And gin I live to keep him sae
 I 'm blest aboon the lave:
And will I see his face again?
 And will I hear him speak?
I 'm downright dizzy wi' the thought,
 In troth I 'm like to greet.
For there 's nae luck about the house,
 There 's nae luck at a';
There 's little pleasure in the house
 When our gudeman 's awa'.          56

1769.                          *W. J. Mickle.*


# LOCHINVAR

### LADY HERON'S SONG

From *Marmion*

OH! young Lochinvar is come out of the west,
Through all the wide Border his steed was the
    best;
And save his good broadsword he weapons had
    none,
He rode all unarmed and he rode all alone.
So faithful in love and so dauntless in war,
There never was knight like the young Lochin-
    var.                                          6

# Lochinvar

He stayed not for brake and he stopped not for
    stone,
He swam the Eske river where ford there was
    none;
But ere he alighted at Netherby gate
The bride had consented, the gallant came late:
For a laggard in love and a dastard in war
Was to wed the fair Ellen of brave Lochin-
    var.          12


So boldly he entered the Netherby Hall,
Among bridesmen, and kinsmen, and brothers,
    and all:
Then spoke the bride's father, his hand on his
    sword,—
For the poor craven bridegroom said never a
    word,—
"Oh! come ye in peace here, or come ye in war,
Or to dance at our bridal, young Lord Lochin-
    var?"—        18


"I long wooed your daughter, my suit you denied;
Love swells like the Solway, but ebbs like its
    tide—
And now am I come, with this lost love of mine,
To lead but one measure, drink one cup of wine.
There are maidens in Scotland more lovely by
    far,
That would gladly be bride to the young Loch-
    invar."       24

The bride kissed the goblet; the knight took it
    up,
He quaffed off the wine, and he threw down the
    cup.
She looked down to blush, and she looked up to
    sigh,
With a smile on her lips and a tear in her eye.
He took her soft hand ere her mother could
    bar,—
"Now tread we a measure!" said young Loch-
    invar.        30

So stately his form, and so lovely her face,
That never a hall such a galliard did grace;
While her mother did fret, and her father did
    fume,
And the bridegroom stood dangling his bonnet
    and plume;
And the bride-maidens whispered, "'T were
    better by far
To have matched our fair cousin with young
    Lochinvar."        36

One touch to her hand and one word in her ear,
When they reached the hall-door, and the
    charger stood near;
So light to the croupe the fair lady he swung,
So light to the saddle before her he sprung!
"She is won! we are gone, over bank, bush, and
    scaur;
They'll have fleet steeds that follow," quoth
    young Lochinvar.        42

### The Maid of Neidpath

There was mounting 'mong Græmes of the
    Netherby clan;
Forsters, Fenwicks, and Musgraves, they rode
    and they ran:
There was racing and chasing on Cannobie Lee,
But the lost bride of Netherby ne'er did they
    see.
So daring in love and so dauntless in war,
Have ye e'er heard of gallant like young Loch-
    invar?        48

1808.            *Sir Walter Scott.*


## THE MAID OF NEIDPATH

O, LOVERS' eyes are sharp to see,
    And lovers' ears in hearing;
And love in life's extremity
    Can lend an hour of cheering.
Disease had been in Mary's bower,
    And slow decay from mourning,
Though now she sits on Neidpath's tower
    To watch her love's returning.    8

All sunk and dim her eyes so bright,
    Her form decayed by pining,
Till through her wasted hand at night
    You saw the taper shining;

By fits, a sultry hectic hue
    Across her cheek was flying;
By fits, so ashy pale she grew,
    Her maidens thought her dying.    16

Yet keenest powers to see and hear
    Seemed in her frame residing;
Before the watch-dog pricked his ear,
    She heard her lover's riding;
Ere scarce a distant form was kenned,
    She knew, and waved to greet him;
And o'er the battlement did bend,
    As on the wing to meet him.    24

He came—he passed—an heedless gaze,
    As o'er some stranger glancing;
Her welcome, spoke in faltering phrase,
    Lost in his courser's prancing—
The castle arch, whose hollow tone
    Returns each whisper spoken,
Could scarcely catch the feeble moan
    Which told her heart was broken.    32

1806.                *Sir Walter Scott.*


# A WEARY LOT IS THINE

### From *Rokeby*

"A WEARY lot is thine, fair maid,
    A weary lot is thine!
To pull the thorn thy brow to braid,
    And press the rue for wine!

# Brignall Banks

A lightsome eye, a soldier's mien,
    A feather of the blue,
A doublet of the Lincoln green,—
    No more of me you knew,
       My love!
    No more of me you knew.      10

"This morn is merry June, I trow,
    The rose is budding fain;
But she shall bloom in winter snow
    Ere we two meet again."
He turn'd his charger as he spake
    Upon the river shore,
He gave the bridle-reins a shake,
    Said "Adieu for evermore,
       My love!
    And adieu for evermore."      20

*Sir Walter Scott.*

1813.


# BRIGNALL BANKS

### From *Rokeby*

O, BRIGNALL banks are wild and fair,
    And Greta woods are green,
And you may gather garlands there
    Would grace a summer queen.
And as I rode by Dalton-hall,
    Beneath the turrets high,

A maiden on the castle wall
   Was singing merrily,—
"O, Brignall banks are fresh and fair,
   And Greta woods are green;
I'd rather rove with Edmund there
   Than reign our English queen."    12

"If, maiden, thou wouldst wend with me,
   To leave both tower and town,
Thou first must guess what life lead we
   That dwell by dale and down.
And if thou canst that riddle read,
   As read full well you may,
Then to the greenwood shalt thou speed,
   As blithe as Queen of May."
Yet sung she, "Brignall banks are fair,
   And Greta woods are green;
I'd rather rove with Edmund there
   Than reign our English queen.    24

"I read you, by your bugle horn,
   And by your palfry good,
I read you for a ranger sworn
   To keep the king's greenwood."
"A ranger, lady, winds his horn,
   And 't is at peep of light;
His blast is heard at merry morn,
   And mine at dead of night."
Yet sung she, "Brignall banks are fair,
   And Greta woods are gay;
I would I were with Edmund there,
   To reign his Queen of May!    36

# Brignall Banks

"With burnished brand and musketoon
    So gallantly you come,
I read you for a bold dragoon,
    That lists the tuck of drum."
"I list no more the tuck of drum,
    No more the trumpet hear;
But when the beetle sounds his hum,
    My comrades take the spear.
And O, though Brignall banks be fair,
    And Greta woods be gay,
Yet mickle must the maiden dare
    Would reign my Queen of May!        48


"Maiden! a nameless life I lead,
    A nameless death I 'll die;
The fiend whose lantern lights the mead
    Were better mate than I!
And when I 'm with my comrades met
    Beneath the greenwood bough,
What once we were we all forget,
    Nor think what we are now.
Yet Brignall banks are fresh and fair,
    And Greta woods are green,
And you may gather garlands there
    Would grace a summer queen."        60

1813.                              *Sir Walter Scott.*

# LOVE

ALL thoughts, all passions, all delights,
Whatever stirs this mortal frame,
All are but ministers of Love,
    And feed his sacred flame.       4

Oft in my waking dreams do I
Live o'er again that happy hour,
When midway on the mount I lay,
    Beside the ruined tower.       8

The moonshine, stealing o'er the scene
Had blended with the lights of eve;
And she was there, my hope, my joy,
    My own dear Genevieve!       12

She leant against the armèd man,
The statue of the armèd knight;
She stood and listened to my lay,
    Amid the lingering light.       16

Few sorrows hath she of her own.
My hope! my joy! my Genevieve!
She loves me best, whene'er I sing
    The songs that make her grieve.       20

# Love

I played a soft and doleful air,
I sang an old and moving story—
An old rude song, that suited well
    That ruin wild and hoary.     24

She listened with a flitting blush,
With downcast eyes and modest grace;
For well she knew, I could not choose
    But gaze upon her face.     28

I told her of the Knight that wore
Upon his shield a burning brand;
And that for ten long years he wooed
    The Lady of the Land.     32

I told her how he pined: and ah!
The deep, the low, the pleading tone
With which I sang another's love,
    Interpreted my own.     36

She listened with a flitting blush,
With downcast eyes and modest grace;
And she forgave me that I gazed
    Too fondly on her face!     40

But when I told the cruel scorn
That crazed that bold and lovely Knight,
And that he crossed the mountain-woods,
    Nor rested day nor night;     44

That sometimes from the savage den,
And sometimes from the darksome shade,

And sometimes starting up at once
   In green and sunny glade,—    48

There came and looked him in the face
An angel beautiful and bright;
And that he knew it was a Fiend,
   This miserable Knight!    56

And that unknowing what he did,
He leaped amid a murderous band,
And saved from outrage worse than death
   The Lady of the Land!    56

And how she wept, and clasped his knees;
And how she tended him in vain—
And ever strove to expiate
   The scorn that crazed his brain;—    60

And that she nursed him in a cave;
And how his madness went away,
When on the yellow forest-leaves
   A dying man he lay;—    64

His dying words—but when I reached
That tenderest strain of all the ditty,
My faultering voice and pausing harp
   Disturbed her soul with pity!    68

All impulses of soul and sense
Had thrilled my guileless Genevieve;
The music and the doleful tale,
   The rich and balmy eve;    72

# Love

And hopes, and fears that kindle hope,
An undistinguishable throng,
And gentle wishes long subdued,
    Subdued and cherished long!    76

She wept with pity and delight,
She blushed with love, and virgin shame;
And like the murmur of a dream,
    I heard her breathe my name.    80

Her bosom heaved—she stepped aside,
As conscious of my look she stepped—
Then suddenly, with timorous eye
    She fled to me and wept.    84

She half enclosed me with her arms,
She pressed me with a meek embrace;
And bending back her head, looked up,
    And gazed upon my face.    88

'T was partly love, and partly fear,
And partly 't was a bashful art,
That I might rather feel, than see,
    The swelling of her heart.    92

I calmed her fears, and she was calm,
And told her love with virgin pride;
And so I won my Genevieve,
    My bright and beauteous Bride.    96

1799.                  *Samuel Taylor Coleridge.*

# GLENKINDIE

ABOUT Glenkindie and his man,
  A false ballant hath long been writ;
  Some bootless loon had written it,
Upon a bootless plan:
But I have found the true at last,
And here it is, so hold it fast.
'T was made by a kind damosel
Who loved him and his man right well.   8

------

Glenkindie, best of harpers, came
  Unbidden to our town;
And he was sad, and sad to see,
  For love had worn him down.   12

It was love, as all men know,
  The love that brought him down,
The hopeless love for the king's daughter,
  The dove that heir'd a crown.   16

Now he wore not that collar of gold,
  His dress was forest green,
His wondrous fair and rich mantel
  Had lost its silvery sheen.   20

# Glenkindie

But still by his side walked Rafe, his boy,
   In goodly cramoisie:
Of all the boys that ever I saw,
   The goodliest boy was he.     24


O Rafe the page! O Rafe the page!
   Ye stole the heart frae me:
O Rafe the page! O Rafe the page!
   I wonder where ye be;
We ne'er may see Glenkindie more,
   But may we never see thee?     30


Glenkindie came within the hall,
   We set him on the dais,
And gave him bread, and gave him wine,
   The best in all the place.     34


We set for him the guests' high chair,
   And spread the naperie:
Our Dame herself would serve for him,
   And I for Rafe, perdie!     38


But down he sat on a low, low stool
   And thrust his long legs out,
And leant his back to the high chair,
   And turn'd his harp about.     42


He turn'd it round, he strok'd the strings,
   He touch'd each tirling-pin,
He put his mouth to the sounding-board
   And breath'd his breath therein.     46

And Rafe sat over against his face,
    And look'd at him wistfullie:
I almost grat ere he began,
    They were so sad to see.        50

The very first stroke he strack that day
    We all came crowding near;
And the second stroke he strack that day
    We all were smit with fear.     54

The third stroke that he strack that day
    Full fain we were to cry;
The fourth stroke that he strack that day
    We thought that we would die.     58

No tongue can tell how sweet it was,
    How far and yet how near,
We saw the saints in Paradise,
    And bairnies on their bier.     62

And our sweet Dame saw her good lord—
    She told me privilie—
She saw him as she saw him last,
    On his ship upon the sea.     66

Anon he laid his little harp by,
    He shut his wondrous eyes;
We stood a long time like dumb things,
    Stood in a dumb surprise.     70

Then all at once we left that trance,
    And shouted where we stood;

We clasp'd each other's hands and vow'd
    We would be wise and good.      74

Soon he rose up and Rafe rose too,
    He drank wine and broke bread;
He clasp'd his hands with our trembling
      Dame,
    But never a word he said.
They went,—Alack and lack-a-day!
    They went the way they came.      80

I follow'd them all down the floor,
    And oh but I had drouth
To touch his cheek, to touch his hand,
    To kiss Rafe's velvet mouth!      84

But I knew such was not for me.
    They went straight from the door;
We saw them fade within the mist,
    And never saw them more.      88

1882.           *William Bell Scott.*

# SIR LAUNCELOT AND QUEEN GUINEVERE

LIKE souls that balance joy and pain,
With tears and smiles from heaven again
The maiden Spring upon the plain
Came in a sun-lit fall of rain.
    In crystal vapour everywhere

51

Blue isles of heaven laugh'd between,
And far, in forest-deeps unseen,
The topmost elm-tree gather'd green
   From draughts of balmy air.     9

Sometimes the linnet piped his song:
Sometimes the throstle whistled strong:
Sometimes the sparhawk, wheel'd along,
Hush'd all the groves from fear of wrong:
   By grassy capes with fuller sound
In curves the yellowing river ran,
And drooping chestnut-buds began
To spread into the perfect fan,
   Above the teeming ground.     18

Then, in the boyhood of the year,
Sir Launcelot and Queen Guinevere
Rode thro' the coverts of the deer,
With blissful treble ringing clear.
   She seem'd a part of joyous Spring:
A gown of grass-green silk she wore,
Buckled with golden clasps before;
A light-green tuft of plumes she bore
   Closed in a golden ring.     27

Now on some twisted ivy-net,
Now by some tinkling rivulet,
In mosses mixt with violet
Her cream-white mule his pastern set:
   And fleeter now she skimm'd the plains
Than she whose elfin prancer springs
By night to eery warblings,

## Amy Wentworth

When all the glimmering moorland rings
  With jingling bridle-reins.      36

As fast she fled thro' sun and shade,
The happy winds upon her play'd,
Blowing the ringlet from the braid:
She look'd so lovely, as she sway'd
  The rein with dainty finger-tips,
A man had given all other bliss,
And all his worldly worth for this,
To waste his whole heart in one kiss
  Upon her perfect lips.      45

1842.                           *Lord Tennyson.*


## AMY WENTWORTH

HER fingers shame the ivory keys
  They dance so light along;
The bloom upon her parted lips
  Is sweeter than the song.      4

O perfumed suitor, spare thy smiles!
  Her thoughts are not of thee;
She better loves the salted wind,
  The voices of the sea.      8

Her heart is like an outbound ship
  That at its anchor swings;
The murmur of the stranded shell
  Is in the song she sings.      12

She sings, and, smiling, hears her praise,
　But dreams the while of one
Who watches from his sea-blown deck
　The icebergs in the sun.　　　　　16

She questions all the winds that blow,
　And every fog-wreath dim,
And bids the sea-birds flying north
　Bear messages to him.　　　　　20

She speeds them with the thanks of men
　He perilled life to save,
And grateful prayers like holy oil
　To smooth for him the wave.　　　24

Brown Viking of the fishing-smack!
　Fair toast of all the town!—
The skipper's jerkin ill beseems
　The lady's silken gown!　　　　　28

But ne'er shall Amy Wentworth wear
　For him the blush of shame
Who dares to set his manly gifts
　Against her ancient name.　　　　32

The stream is brightest at its spring,
　And blood is not like wine;
Nor honored less than he who heirs
　Is he who founds a line.　　　　　36

Full lightly shall the prize be won,
　If love be Fortune's spur;

# Amy Wentworth

And never maiden stoops to him
  Who lifts himself to her.     40

Her home is brave in Jaffrey Street,
  With stately stairways worn
By feet of old Colonial knights
  And ladies gentle-born.     44

Still green about its ample porch
  The English ivy twines,
Trained back to show in English oak
  The herald's carven signs.     48

And on her, from the wainscot old,
  Ancestral faces frown,—
And this has worn the soldier's sword,
  And that the judge's gown.     52

But, strong of will and proud as they,
  She walks the gallery floor
As if she trod on sailor's deck
  By stormy Labrador!     56

The sweetbrier blooms on Kittery-side,
  And green are Elliot's bowers;
Her garden is the pebbled beach,
  The mosses are her flowers.     60

She looks across the harbor-bar
  To see the white gulls fly;
His greeting from the Northern sea
  Is in their clanging cry.     64

She hums a song, and dreams that he,
    As in its romance old,
Shall homeward ride with silken sails
    And masts of beaten gold!    68

Oh, rank is good, and gold is fair,
    And high and low mate ill;
But love has never known a law
    Beyond its own sweet will!    72

*1862.*               *John Greenleaf Whittier.*


# ANNABEL LEE

It was many and many a year ago,
    In a kingdom by the sea,
That a maiden there lived whom you may know
    By the name of Annabel Lee;
And this maiden she lived with no other thought
    Than to love and be loved by me.    6

I was a child and *she* was a child,
    In this kingdom by the sea:
But we loved with a love that was more than
        love—
    I and my Annabel Lee;
With a love that the wingèd seraphs of heaven
    Coveted her and me.    12

And this was the reason that, long ago,
    In this kingdom by the sea,

# Annabel Lee

A wind blew out of a cloud, chilling
    My beautiful Annabel Lee;
So that her high-born kinsman came
    And bore her away from me,
To shut her up in a sepulchre
    In this kingdom by the sea.     20

The angels, not half so happy in heaven,
    Went envying her and me—
Yes! that was the reason (as all men know,
    In this kingdom by the sea)
That the wind came out of the cloud by night,
    Chilling and killing my Annabel Lee.     26

But our love it was stronger by far than the love
    Of those who were older than we—
    Of many far wiser than we—
And neither the angels in heaven above,
    Nor the demons down under the sea,
Can ever dissever my soul from the soul
    Of the beautiful Annabel Lee,     33

For the moon never beams, without bringing me
      dreams
    Of the beautiful Annabel Lee;
And the stars never rise, but I feel the bright eyes
    Of the beautiful Annabel Lee;
And so, all the night-tide, I lie down by the side
Of my darling—my darling—my life and my
      bride,
    In the sepulchre there by the sea,
    In her tomb by the sounding sea.     41

1849.              *Edgar Allan Poe.*

# THE BLESSED DAMOZEL

THE blessed Damozel lean'd out
   From the gold bar of Heaven:
Her blue grave eyes were deeper much
   Than a deep water, even.
She had three lilies in her hand,
   And the stars in her hair were seven.    **6**

Her robe, ungirt from clasp to hem,
   No wrought flowers did adorn,
But a white rose of Mary's gift
   On the neck meetly worn;
And her hair, lying down her back,
   Was yellow like ripe corn.    **12**

Herseem'd she scarce had been a day
   One of God's choristers;
The wonder was not yet quite gone
   From that still look of hers;
Albeit, to them she left, her day
   Had counted as ten years.    **18**

(To *one* it is ten years of years:
   . . . Yet now, here in this place,
Surely she lean'd o'er me,—her hair
   Fell all about my face. . . .

# The Blessed Damozel

Nothing: the Autumn-fall of leaves.
   The whole year sets apace.)      24


It was the terrace of God's house
   That she was standing on,—
By God built over the sheer depth
   In which Space is begun;
So high, that looking downward thence,
   She scarce could see the sun.      30


It lies from Heaven across the flood
   Of ether, as a bridge.
Beneath, the tides of day and night
   With flame and blackness ridge
The void, as low as where this earth
   Spins like a fretful midge.      36


But in those tracts, with her, it was
   The peace of utter light
And silence. For no breeze may stir
   Along the steady flight
Of seraphim; no echo there,
   Beyond all depth or height.      42


Heard hardly, some of her new friends,
   Playing at holy games,
Spake, gentle-mouth'd, among themselves,
   Their virginal chaste names;
And the souls, mounting up to God,
   Went by her like thin flames.      48

And still she bow'd herself, and stoop'd
    Into the vast waste calm;
Till her bosom's pressure must have made
    The bar she lean'd on warm,
And the lilies lay as if asleep
    Along her bended arm.                    54

From the fixt lull of Heaven, she saw
    Time, like a pulse, shake fierce
Through all the worlds.  Her gaze still strove,
    In that steep gulf, to pierce
The swarm: and then she spake, as when
    The stars sang in their spheres.         60

"I wish that he were come to me,
    For he will come," she said.
"Have I not pray'd in solemn Heaven?
    On earth, has he not pray'd?
Are not two prayers a perfect strength?
    And shall I feel afraid?                 66

"When round his head the aureole clings,
    And he is clothed in white,
I 'll take his hand, and go with him ·
    To the deep wells of light,
And we will step down as to a stream
    And bathe there in God's sight.          72

"We two will stand beside that shrine,
    Occult, withheld, untrod,
Whose lamps tremble continually
    With prayer sent up to God;

And where each need, reveal'd, expects
    Its patient period.        78


" We two will lie i' the shadow of
    That living mystic tree
Within whose secret growth the Dove
    Sometimes is felt to be,
While every leaf that His plumes touch
    Saith His name audibly.       84


" And I myself will teach to him, —
    I myself, lying so, —
The songs I sing here; which his mouth
    Shall pause in, hush'd and slow,
Finding some knowledge at each pause,
    And some new thing to know."    90


(Alas! to her wise simple mind
    These things were all but known
Before: they trembled on her sense, —
    Her voice had caught their tone.
Alas for lonely Heaven! Alas
    For life wrung out alone!      96


Alas, and though the end were reach'd? . . .
    Was thy part understood
Or borne in trust? And for her sake
    Shall this too be found good? —
May the close lips that knew not prayer
    Praise ever, though they would?)    102

"We *two*," she said, "will seek the groves
    Where the lady Mary is,
With her five handmaidens, whose names
    Are five sweet symphonies:—
Cecily, Gertrude, Magdalen,
    Margaret and Rosalys.    108

"Circle-wise sit they, with bound locks
    And bosoms covered;
Into the fine cloth, white like flame,
    Weaving the golden thread,
To fashion the birth-robes for them
    Who are just born, being dead.    114

"He shall fear haply, and be dumb.
    Then I will lay my cheek
To his, and tell about our love,
    Not once abash'd or weak:
And the dear Mother will approve
    My pride, and let me speak.    120

"Herself shall bring us, hand in hand,
    To Him round whom all souls
Kneel—the unnumber'd solemn heads
    Bow'd with their aureoles:
And Angels, meeting us, shall sing
    To their citherns and citoles.    126

"There will I ask of Christ the Lord
    Thus much for him and me:—
To have more blessing than on earth
    In nowise; but to be

# The Blessed Damozel

As then we were,—being as then
    At peace. Yea, verily.        132

"Yea, verily; when he is come
    We will do thus and thus:
Till this my vigil seem quite strange
    And almost fabulous;
We two will live at once, one life;
    And peace shall be with us."      138

She gazed, and listened, and then said,
    Less sad of speech than mild,—
"All this is when he comes." She ceased:
    The light thrill'd past her, fill'd
With Angels, in strong level lapse.
    Her eyes pray'd, and she smiled.    144

(I saw her smile.) But soon their flight
    Was vague 'mid the poised spheres.
And then she cast her arms along
    The golden barriers,
And laid her face between her hands,
    And wept. (I heard her tears.)    150

1850.             *Dante Gabriel Rossetti.*

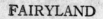

FAIRYLAND

# THOMAS THE RHYMER

TRUE Thomas lay on Huntlie bank;
  A ferlie he spied wi' his e'e;
And there he saw a ladye bright
  Come riding down by the Eildon Tree. 4

Her skirt was o' the grass-green silk,
  Her mantle o' the velvet fine;
At ilka tett o' her horse's mane,
  Hung fifty siller bells and nine. 8

True Thomas, he pu'd aff his cap,
  And louted low down on his knee:
"Hail to thee, Mary, Queen of Heaven!
  For thy peer on earth could never be." 12

"O no, O no, Thomas," she said,
  "That name does not belang to me;
I 'm but the Queen o' fair Elfland,
  That am hither come to visit thee. 16

"Harp and carp, Thomas," she said;
  "Harp and carp along wi' me;
And if ye dare to kiss my lips,
  Sure of your bodie I will be." 20

67

"Betide me weal, betide me woe,
    That weird shall never daunten me."
Syne he has kiss'd her rosy lips,
    All underneath the Eildon Tree.          24


"Now ye maun go wi' me," she said,
    "True Thomas, ye maun go wi' me;
And ye maun serve me seven years,
    Thro' weal or woe as may chance to be."  28


She's mounted on her milk-white steed,
    She's ta'en true Thomas up behind;
And aye, whene'er her bridle rang,
    The steed gaed swifter than the wind.    30


O they rade on, and farther on,
    The steed gaed swifter than the wind;
Until they reach'd a desert wide,
    And living land was left behind.         36


"Light down, light down, now, true Thomas,
    And lean your head upon my knee;
Abide ye there a little space,
    And I will show you ferlies three.       40


"O see ye not yon narrow road,
    So thick beset wi' thorns and briers?
That is the path of righteousness,
    Though after it but few inquires.        44


"And see ye not yon braid, braid road,
    That lies across the lily leven?

# Thomas the Rhymer

That is the path of wickedness,
    Though some call it the road to
      Heaven.      48

"And see ye not yon bonny road
    That winds about the fernie brae?
That is the road to fair Elfland,
    Where thou and I this night maun gae. 52

"But, Thomas, ye sall haud your tongue,
    Whatever ye may hear or see;
For speak ye word in Elflyn-land,
    Ye'll ne'er win back to your ain coun-
      trie."      56

O they rade on, and farther on,
    And they waded rivers abune the knee;
And they saw neither sun nor moon,
    But they heard the roaring of the sea.  60

It was mirk, mirk night, there was nae
    sternlight,
    They waded thro' red blude to the knee;
For a' the blude that's shed on the earth
    Rins through the springs o' that coun-
      trie.      64

Syne they came on to a garden green,
    And she pu'd an apple frae a tree:
"Take this for thy wages, true Thomas;
    It will give thee the tongue that can
      never lie."      68

"My tongue is mine ain," true Thomas he
    said;
  "A gudely gift ye wad gie to me!
I neither dought to buy or sell
    At fair or tryst where I might be.   72

"I dought neither speak to prince or peer,
    Nor ask of grace from fair ladye!"—
"Now haud thy peace, Thomas," she said,
  "For as I say, so must it be."   76

He has gotten a coat of the even cloth,
    And a pair of shoon of the velvet green;
And till seven years were gane and past,
    True Thomas on earth was never seen. 80

             *Scott, Minst. Scot. Bord.*

## KEMP OWYNE

HER mother died when she was young,
  Which gave her cause to make great moan;
Her father married the warst woman
    That ever lived in Christendom.

She served her with foot and hand,   5
  In everything that she could dee,
Till once, in an unlucky time,
    She threw her in o'er Craigy's sea.

Says, "Lie you there, dove Isabel,
  And all my sorrows lie with thee;   10

# Kemp Owyne

Till Kemp Owyne come o'er the sea,
    And borrow you with kisses three,
Let all the warld do what they will,
    Oh, borrowed shall you never be!"

Her breath grew strang, her hair grew lang,   15
    And twisted thrice about the tree,
And all the people, far and near,
    Thought that a savage beast was she.

These news did come to Kemp Owyne,
    Where he lived, far beyond the sea;   20
He hasted him to Craigy's sea,
    And on the savage beast looked he.

Her breath was strang, her hair was lang,
    And twisted was about the tree,
And with a swing she came about:   25
    "Come to Craigy's sea, and kiss with me.

"Here is a royal belt," she cried,
    "That I have found in the green sea;
And while your body it is on,
    Drawn shall your blood never be;   30
But if you touch me, tail or fin,
    I vow my belt your death shall be."

He stepped in, gave her a kiss,
    The royal belt he brought him wi';
Her breath was strang, her hair was lang,   35
    And twisted twice about the tree,

And with a swing she came about:
"Come to Craigy's sea, and kiss with me.

"Here is a royal ring," she said,
  "That I have found in the green sea;        40
And while your finger it is on,
  Drawn shall your blood never be;
But if you touch me, tail or fin,
  I swear my ring your death shall be."

He stepped in, gave her a kiss,            45
  The royal ring he brought him wi';
Her breath was strang, her hair was lang,
  And twisted ance about the tree,
And with a swing she came about:
  "Come to Craigy's sea, and kiss with me.   50

"Here is a royal brand," she said,
  "That I have found in the green sea;
And while your body it is on,
  Drawn shall your blood never be;
But if you touch me, tail or fin,          55
  I swear my brand your death shall be."

He stepped in, gave her a kiss,
  The royal brand he brought him wi';
Her breath was sweet, her hair grew short,
  And twisted nane about the tree,          60
And smilingly she came about,
  As fair a woman as fair could be.

                    *Child, Pop. Bal., No. 34A.*

# THE LADY OF SHALOTT

## PART I

On either side the river lie
Long fields of barley and of rye,
That clothe the wold and meet the sky;
And thro' the field the road runs by
    To many-tower'd Camelot;
And up and down the people go,
Gazing where the lilies blow
Round an island there below,
    The island of Shalott.                    9

Willows whiten, aspens quiver,
Little breezes dusk and shiver
Thro' the wave that runs for ever
By the island in the river
    Flowing down to Camelot.
Four gray walls, and four gray towers,
Overlook a space of flowers,
And the silent isle imbowers
    The Lady of Shalott.                    18

By the margin, willow-veil'd,
Slide the heavy barges trail'd

By slow horses; and unhail'd
The shallop flitteth silken-sail'd
      Skimming down to Camelot:
But who hath seen her wave her hand?
Or at the casement seen her stand?
Or is she known in all the land,
      The Lady of Shalott?       **27**

Only reapers, reaping early
In among the bearded barley,
Hear a song that echoes cheerly
From the river winding clearly,
      Down to tower'd Camelot:
And by the moon the reaper weary,
Piling sheaves in uplands airy,
Listening, whispers " 'T is the fairy
      Lady of Shalott."       **36**

### PART II

There she weaves by night and day
A magic web with colours gay.
She has heard a whisper say,
A curse is on her if she stay
      To look down to Camelot.
She knows not what the curse may be,
And so she weaveth steadily,
And little other care hath she,
      The Lady of Shalott.       **45**

And moving thro' a mirror clear
That hangs before her all the year,

# The Lady of Shalott

Shadows of the world appear.
There she sees the highway near
    Winding down to Camelot:
There the river eddy whirls,
And there the surly village-churls,
And the red cloaks of market-girls,
    Pass onward from Shalott.    54

Sometimes a troop of damsels glad,
An abbot on an ambling pad,
Sometimes a curly shepherd-lad,
Or long-hair'd page in crimson clad,
    Goes by to tower'd Camelot:
And sometimes thro' the mirror blue
The knights come riding two and two:
She hath no loyal knight and true,
    The Lady of Shalott.    63

But in her web she still delights
To weave the mirror's magic sights,
For often thro' the silent nights
A funeral, with plumes and lights
    And music, went to Camelot:
Or when the moon was overhead,
Came two young lovers lately wed;
"I am half sick of shadows," said
    The Lady of Shalott.    72

## PART III

A bow-shot from her bower-eaves,
He rode between the barley-sheaves,

The sun came dazzling thro' the leaves,
And flamed upon the brazen greaves
     Of bold Sir Lancelot.
A red-cross knight for ever kneel'd
To a lady in his shield,
That sparkled on the yellow field,
     Beside remote Shalott.      81

The gemmy bridle glitter'd free,
Like to some branch of stars we see
Hung in the golden Galaxy.
The bridle bells rang merrily
     As he rode down to Camelot:
And from his blazon'd baldric slung
A mighty silver bugle hung,
And as he rode his armour rung,
     Beside remote Shalott.      90

All in the blue unclouded weather
Thick-jewell'd shone the saddle-leather,
The helmet and the helmet-feather
Burn'd like one burning flame together,
     As he rode down to Camelot.
As often thro' the purple night,
Below the starry clusters bright,
Some bearded meteor, trailing light,
     Moves over still Shalott.      99

His broad clear brow in sunlight glow'd;
On burnish'd hooves his war-horse trode;
From underneath his helmet flow'd
His coal-black curls as on he rode,
     As he rode down to Camelot.

From the bank and from the river
He flash'd into the crystal mirror,
"Tirra lirra," by the river
    Sang Sir Lancelot.        108

She left the web, she left the loom,
She made three paces thro' the room,
She saw the water-lily bloom,
She saw the helmet and the plume,
    She look'd down to Camelot.
Out flew the web and floated wide;
The mirror crack'd from side to side;
"The curse is come upon me," cried
    The Lady of Shalott.        117

### PART IV

In the stormy east-wind straining,
The pale yellow woods were waning,
The broad stream in his banks complaining,
Heavily the low sky raining
    Over tower'd Camelot;
Down she came and found a boat
Beneath a willow left afloat,
And round about the prow she wrote
    *The Lady of Shalott.*        126

And down the river's dim expanse
Like some bold seër in a trance,
Seeing all his own mischance—
With a glassy countenance
    Did she look to Camelot.

And at the closing of the day
She loosed the chain, and down she lay;
The broad stream bore her far away,
  The Lady of Shalott.  135


Lying, robed in snowy white
That loosely flew to left and right—
The leaves upon her falling light—
Thro' the noises of the night
  She floated down to Camelot:
And as the boat-head wound along
The willowy hills and fields among,
They heard her singing her last song,
  The Lady of Shalott.  144


Heard a carol, mournful, holy,
Chanted loudly, chanted lowly,
Till her blood was frozen slowly
And her eyes were darken'd wholly
  Turn'd to tower'd Camelot.
For ere she reach'd upon the tide
The first house by the water-side,
Singing in her song she died,
  The Lady of Shalott.  153


Under tower and balcony,
By garden-wall and gallery,
A gleaming shape she floated by,
Dead-pale between the houses high,
  Silent into Camelot.

Out upon the wharfs they came,
Knight and burgher, lord and dame,
And round the prow they read her name,
   *The Lady of Shalott.*     **162**

Who is this? and what is here?
And in the lighted palace near
Died the sound of royal cheer;
And they cross'd themselves for fear,
   All the knights at Camelot:
But Lancelot mused a little space;
He said, " She has a lovely face;
God in his mercy lend her grace,
   The Lady of Shalott."     **171**

1833.  1842.        *Lord Tennyson.*

# THE ROMANCE OF THE
# SWAN'S NEST

" So the dreams depart,
  So the fading phantoms flee,
  And the sharp reality
Now must act its part."
     WESTWOOD'S *Beads from a Rosary.*

LITTLE Ellie sits alone
  'Mid the beeches of a meadow,
By a stream-side on the grass,
And the trees are showering down
  Doubles of their leaves in shadow     **5**
On her shining hair and face.

She has thrown her bonnet by,
　　And her feet she has been dipping
In the shallow water's flow:
Now she holds them nakedly　　　　　10
　　In her hands, all sleek and dripping,
While she rocketh to and fro.


Little Ellie sits alone,
　　And the smile she softly uses
Fills the silence like a speech,　　　　15
While she thinks what shall be done,
　　And the sweetest pleasure chooses
For her future within reach.


Little Ellie in her smile
　　Chooses—"I will have a lover　　　20
Riding on a steed of steeds:
He shall love me without guile,
　　And to *him* I will discover
The swan's nest among the reeds.


" And the steed shall be red-roan,　　25
　　And the lover shall be noble,
With an eye that takes the breath:
And the lute he plays upon
　　Shall strike ladies into trouble,
As his sword strikes men to death.　　30


" And the steed it shall be shod
　　All in silver, housed in azure,

80

And the mane shall swim the wind;
And the hoofs along the sod
　　Shall flash onward and keep measure,　35
Till the shepherds look behind.

"But my lover will not prize
　　All the glory that he rides in,
When he gazes in my face:
　　He will say, 'O Love, thine eyes　　40
　　Build the shrine my soul abides in,
And I kneel here for thy grace!'

"Then, ay, then he shall kneel low,
　　With the red-roan steed anear him
Which shall seem to understand,　　45
　　Till I answer, 'Rise and go!
　　For the world must love and fear him
Whom I gift with heart and hand.'

"Then he will arise so pale,
　　I shall feel my own lips tremble　50
With a *yes* I must not say,
　　Nathless maiden-brave, 'Farewell,'
　　I will utter, and dissemble—
'Light to-morrow with to-day!'

"Then he 'll ride among the hills　55
　　To the wide world past the river,
There to put away all wrong;
　　To make straight distorted wills,
　　And to empty the broad quiver
Which the wicked bear along.　　60

" Three times shall a young foot-page
    Swim the stream and climb the mountain
And kneel down beside my feet—
' Lo, my master sends this gage,
    Lady, for thy pity's counting!          65
What wilt thou exchange for it?'


" And the first time I will send
    A white rosebud for a guerdon,
And the second time, a glove;
But the third time—I may bend          70
    From my pride, and answer—' Pardon,
If he comes to take my love.'


" Then the young foot-page will run,
    Then my lover will ride faster,
Till he kneeleth at my knee:          75
' I am a duke's eldest son,
    Thousand serfs do call me master,
But, O Love, I love but *thee!*'


" He will kiss me on the mouth
    Then, and lead me as a lover          80
Through the crowds that praise his deeds;
And, when soul-tied by one troth,
    Unto *him* I will discover
That swan's nest among the reeds."


Little Ellie, with her smile          85
    Not yet ended, rose up gaily,

## The Fairies

Tied the bonnet, donned the shoe,
And went homeward, round a mile,
  Just to see, as she did daily,
What more eggs were with the two.     **90**

Pushing through the elm-tree copse,
  Winding up the stream, light-hearted,
Where the osier pathway leads,
Past the boughs she stoops—and stops.
  Lo, the wild swan had deserted,     **95**
And a rat had gnawed the reeds!

Ellie went home sad and slow.
  If she found the lover ever,
With his red-roan steed of steeds,
Sooth I know not; but I know     **100**
  She could never show him—never,
That swan's nest among the reeds!

1844.              *Elizabeth Barrett Browning.*


## THE FAIRIES

Up the airy mountain,
  Down the rushy glen,
We dare n't go a-hunting
  For fear of little men;
Wee folk, good folk,
  Trooping all together;
Green jacket, red cap,
  And white owl's feather!     **8**

Down along the rocky shore
  Some make their home,
They live on crispy pancakes
  Of yellow tide-foam;
Some in the reeds
  Of the black mountain-lake,
With frogs for their watch-dogs,
  All night awake.                    16


High on the hill-top
  The old King sits;
He is now so old and gray
  He's nigh lost his wits.
With a bridge of white mist
  Columbkill he crosses,
On his stately journeys
  From Slieveleague to Rosses;
Or going up with music
  On cold starry nights,
To sup with the Queen
  Of the gay Northern Lights.         28


They stole little Bridget
  For seven years long;
When she came down again
  Her friends were all gone.
They took her lightly back,
  Between the night and morrow,
They thought that she was fast asleep
  But she was dead with sorrow.

## La Belle Dame Sans Merci

They have kept her ever since
  Deep within the lakes,
On a bed of flag-leaves,
  Watching till she wakes.          40

By the craggy hill-side,
  Through the mosses bare,
They have planted thorn-trees
  For pleasure here and there.
Is any man so daring
  As dig them up in spite,
He shall find their sharpest thorns
  In his bed at night.             48

Up the airy mountain,
  Down the rushy glen,
We dare n't go a-hunting
  For fear of little men;
Wee folk, good folk,
  Trooping all together;
Green jacket, red cap,
  And white owl's feather!         56

1877.                    *William Allingham.*


# LA BELLE DAME SANS MERCI

O what can ail thee, knight-at-arms,
  Alone and palely loitering?
The sedge has wither'd from the lake,
  And no birds sing.                4

O what can ail thee, knight-at-arms!
    So haggard and so woe-begone?
The squirrel's granary is full,
    And the harvest's done.                    8


I see a lily on thy brow
    With anguish moist and fever dew,
And on thy cheeks a fading rose
    Fast withereth too.                         12


I met a lady in the meads,
    Full beautiful—a faery's child,
Her hair was long, her foot was light,
    And her eyes were wild.                     16


I made a garland for her head,
    And bracelets too, and fragrant zone;
She look'd at me as she did love,
    And made sweet moan.                        20


I set her on my pacing steed,
    And nothing else saw all day long.
For sidelong would she bend, and sing
    A faery song.                               24


She found me roots of relish sweet,
    And honey wild, and manna dew,
And sure in language strange she said—
"I love thee true."                             29

# La Belle Dame Sans Merci

She took me to her elfin grot,
  And there she wept, and sigh'd full sore,
And there I shut her wild, wild eyes
  With kisses four.                          32

And there she lulled me asleep,
  And there I dream'd—Ah! woe betide
The latest dream I ever dream'd
  On the cold hill's side.                   36

I saw pale kings and princes too,
  Pale warriors, death-pale were they all;
They cried—"La Belle Dame sans Merci
  Hath thee in thrall!"                      40

I saw their starv'd lips in the gloam,
  With horrid warning gaped wide,
And I awoke and found me here,
  On the cold hill's side.                   44

And this is why I sojourn here,
  Alone and palely loitering,
Though the sedge is wither'd from the lake
  And no birds sing.                         48

1820.                                 *John Keats.*

# ADVENTURE

# ROBIN HOOD AND ALLEN-A-DALE

COME, listen to me, you gallants so free,
   All you that loves mirth for to hear,
And I will you tell of a bold outlaw,
   That lived in Nottinghamshire.  (*bis*)   4

As Robin Hood in the forest stood,
   All under the greenwood tree,
There was he ware of a brave young man,
   As fine as fine might be.   8

The youngster was clad in scarlet red,
   In scarlet fine and gay;
And he did frisk it over the plain,
   And chanted a roundelay.   12

As Robin Hood next morning stood
   Amongst the leaves so gay,
There did he espy the same young man
   Come drooping along the way.   16

The scarlet he wore the day before
   It was clean cast away;
And every step he fetched a sigh,
" Alack and well-a-day ! "   20

Then stepped forth brave Little John,
   And Nick, the miller's son;
Which made the young man bend his bow,
   Whenas he see them come.     24

"Stand off! stand off!" the young man said,
   "What is your will with me?"
"You must come before our master straight,
   Under yon greenwood tree."     28

And when he came bold Robin before,
   Robin asked him courteously,
"O hast thou any money to spare
   For my merry men and me?"     32

"I have no money," the young man said,
   "But five shillings and a ring;
And that I have kept this seven long years,
   To have it at my wedding.     36

"Yesterday I should have married a maid,
   But she is now from me ta'en,
And chosen to be an old knight's delight,
   Whereby my poor heart is slain."     40

"What is thy name?" then said Robin Hood,
   "Come tell me without any fail."
"By the faith of my body," then said the young
     man,
   "My name it is Allen-a-Dale."     4

# Robin Hood and Allen-a-Dale

"What wilt thou give me," said Robin Hood,
  "In ready gold or fee,
To help thee to thy true-love again,
  And deliver her unto thee?"     48


"I have no money," then quoth the young man,
  "No ready gold nor fee,
But I will swear upon a book
  Thy true servant for to be."     52


"How many miles is it to thy true-love?
  Come tell me without any guile."
"By the faith of my body," then said the young
    man,
  "It is but five little mile."     56


Then Robin he hasted over the plain,
  He did neither stint nor lin,
Until he came unto the church
  Where Allen should keep his wedding.     60


"What dost thou do here?" the bishop he said,
  "I prithee now to tell me."
"I am a bold harper," quoth Robin Hood,
  "And the best in the north country."     64


"O welcome, O welcome," the bishop he said,
  "That music best pleaseth me."
"You shall have no music," quoth Robin Hood,
  "Till the bride and bridegroom I see."     68

With that came in a wealthy knight,
　Which was both grave and old;
And after him a finikin lass,
　Did shine like glistering gold.　　　72


" This is no fit match," quoth bold Robin
　　Hood,
　" That you do seem to make here;
For since we are come unto the church,
　The bride shall chuse her own dear."　76


Then Robin Hood put his horn to his mouth,
　And blew blasts two or three;
When four-and-twenty bowmen bold
　Came leaping over the lea.　　　80


And when they came into the churchyard,
　Marching all on a row,
The very first man was Allen-a-Dale,
　To give bold Robin his bow.　　　84


" This is thy true-love," Robin he said,
　" Young Allen, as I hear say;
And you shall be married at this same time,
　Before we depart away."　　　88


" That shall not be," the bishop he said,
　" For thy word shall not stand;
They shall be three times asked in the church,
　As the law is of our land."　　　92

Robin Hood pulled off the bishop's coat,
 And put it upon Little John;
"By the faith of my body," then Robin said,
 "This cloth doth make thee a man."   96

When Little John went into the quire,
 The people began for to laugh;
He asked them seven times in the church,
 Lest three times should not be enough.   100

"Who gives me this maid?" then said Little
  John,
 Quoth Robin, "That do I;
And he that doth take her from Allen-a-Dale,
 Full dearly he shall her buy."   104

And thus, having ended the merry wedding,
 The bride looked as fresh as a queen;
And so they returned to the merry greenwood,
 Amongst the leaves so green.   108

      *Child, Pop. Bal., No. 138.*


# ROBIN HOOD AND GUY OF
# GISBORNE

WHEN shales been sheen, and shradds full fair,
 And leaves both large and long,
It is merry, walking in the fair forest,
 To hear the small birds' song.

95

The woodweete sang and would not cease   5
   Amongst the leaves o' lyne;
[So loud, he wakened Robin Hood,
   In the greenwood where he lay.


"Now by my fay," said jolly Robin,
  "A sweven I had this night;]   10
And it is by two wight yeomen,
   By dear God that I mean:


"Methought they did me beat and bind,
   And took my bow me fro':
If I be Robin alive in this land,   15
   I 'll be wrocken on both them two."


"Swevens are swift, master," quoth John,
  "As the wind that blows o'er a hill;
For if it be never so loud this night,
   To-morrow it may be still."   20


"Busk ye, bown ye, my merry men all!
   For John shall go with me;
For I 'll go seek yond wight yeomen
   In greenwood where they be."


They cast on their gown of green;   25
   A-shooting gone are they,
Until they came to the merry greenwood
   Where they had gladdest be;
There were they ware of [a] wight yeoman;
   His body leaned to a tree,   30

A sword and a dagger he wore by his side,
    Had been many a man's bane,
And he was clad in his capul hide,
    Top and tail and mane.

"Stand you still, master," quoth Little John,   35
    "Under this trusty tree,
And I will go to yond wight yeoman
    To know his meaning truly."

"A, John! by me thou sets no store,
    And that's a farly thing;       40
How oft send I my men before,
    And tarry myself behind?

"It is no cunning a knave to ken,
    An a man but hear him speak;
An it were not for bursting of my bow,   45
    John, I would thy head break."

But often words they breeden bale;
    That parted Robin and John;
John is gone to Barnesdale,
    The gates he knows each one.   50

And when he came to Barnesdale,
    Great heaviness there he had;
He found two of his own fellows
    Were slain both in a slade,

And Scarlet afoot flying was     55
    Over stocks and stone,

For the sheriff with seven score men
    Fast after him is gone.

"Yet one shot I 'll shoot," says Little John,
    "With Christ his might and main;      60
I 'll make yond fellow that flies so fast
    To be both glad and fain."

John bent up a good yew bow,
    And fettled him to shoot;
The bow was made of a tender bough,      65
    And fell down to his foot.

"Woe worth thee, wicked wood!" said Little
    John,
  "That e'er thou grew on a tree!
For this day thou art my bale,
    My boot when thou should be!"      70

This shot it was but loosely shot,
    The arrow flew in vain,
And it met one of the sheriff's men:
    Good William o' Trent was slain.

It had been better for William o' Trent      75
    To hang upon a gallow,
Than for to lie in the greenwood,
    There slain with an arrow.

And it is said, when men be met,
    Six can do more than three;      80
And they have ta'en Little John,
    And bound him fast to a tree.

# Robin Hood and Guy of Gisborne

"Thou shalt be drawn by dale and down," quoth
    the sheriff,
  "And hanged high on a hill."
"But thou may fail," quoth Little John,    85
  "If it be Christ's own will."

Let us leave talking of Little John,
  For he is bound fast to a tree,
And talk of Guy and Robin Hood
  In the greenwood where they be;    90

How these two yeomen together they met
  Under the leaves of lyne,
To see what merchandise they made
  Even at that same time.

"Good morrow, good fellow!" quoth Sir Guy; 95
  "Good morrow, good fellow!" quoth he;
"Methinks by this bow thou bears in thy hand,
  A good archer thou seems to be."

"I am wilful of my way," quoth Sir Guy,
  "And of my morning tide."    100
"I'll lead thee through the wood," quoth Robin,
  "Good fellow, I'll be thy guide."

"I seek an outlaw," quoth Sir Guy;
  "Men call him Robin Hood;
I had rather meet with him upon a day    105
  Than forty pounds of gold."

"If you two met, it would be seen whether were
    better
    Afore ye did part away;
Let us some other pastime find,
    Good fellow, I thee pray.         110

"Let us some other masteries make,
    And we will walk in the woods even,
We may chance meet with Robin Hood
    At some unset steven."

They cut them down the summer shroggs   115
    Which grew both under a brier,
And set them three score rood in twin
    To shoot the prickes full near.

"Lead on, good fellow," said Sir Guy,
    "Lead on, I do bid thee."         120
"Nay, by my faith," quoth Robin Hood,
    "The leader thou shalt be."

The first good shot that Robin led,
    Did not shoot an inch the pricke fro'.
Guy was an archer good enough,     125
    But he could ne'er shoot so.

The second shot Sir Guy shot,
    He shot within the garland;
But Robin Hood shot it better than he,
    For he clove the good pricke-wand.     130

# Robin Hood and Guy of Gisborne

"God's blessing on thy heart!" says Guy,
  "Good fellow, thy shooting is good;
For an thy heart be as good as thy hands,
  Thou were better than Robin Hood.

"Tell me thy name, good fellow," quoth Guy, 135
  "Under the leaves of lyne."
"Nay, by my faith," quoth good Robin,
  "Till thou have told me thine."

"I dwell by dale and down," quoth Guy,
  "And I have done many a curst turn; 140
And he that calls me by my right name,
  Calls me Guy of good Gisborne."

"My dwelling is in the wood," says Robin;
  "By thee I set right nought;
My name is Robin Hood of Barnesdale, 145
  A fellow thou has long sought."

He that had neither been a kith nor kin
  Might have seen a full fair sight,
To see how together these yeomen went
  With blades both brown and bright; 150

To have seen how these yeomen together fought
  Two hours of a summer's day:
It was neither Guy nor Robin Hood
  That fettled them to fly away.

Robin was rechless on a root, 155
  And stumbled at that tide;

And Guy was quick and nimble withal,
    And hit him o'er the left side.

"Ah, dear Lady!" said Robin Hood,
    "Thou art both mother and may!     160
I think it was never man's destiny
    To die before his day."

Robin thought on our Lady dear,
    And soon leapt up again;
And thus he came with an awkward stroke; 165
    Good Sir Guy he has slain.

He took Sir Guy's head by the hair,
    And sticked it on his bow's end;
"Thou hast been traitor all thy life,
    Which thing must have an end."     170

Robin pulled forth an Irish knife,
    And knicked Sir Guy in the face,
That he was never on a woman born
    Could tell who Sir Guy was:

Says, "Lie there, lie there, good Sir Guy,     175
    And with me be not wroth;
If thou have had the worse strokes at my hand,
    Thou shalt have the better cloth."

Robin did [off] his gown of green,
    [On] Sir Guy he did it throw;     180
And he put on that capul hide
    That clad him top to toe.

"Thy bow, thy arrows, and little horn,
  With me now I'll bear;
For now I will go to Barnesdale,     185
  To see how my men do fare."


Robin set Guy's horn to his mouth;
  A loud blast in it he did blow.
That beheard the sheriff of Nottingham
  As he leaned under a low;     190


"Hearken! hearken!" said the sheriff,
  "I heard no tidings but good;
For yonder I hear Sir Guy's horn blow,
  For he hath slain Robin Hood:


"For yonder I hear Sir Guy's horn blow,    195
  It blows so well in tide,
For yonder comes that wighty yeoman,
  Clad in his capul hide.


"Come hither, thou good Sir Guy!
  Ask of me what thou wilt have!"    200
"I'll none of thy gold," says Robin Hood,
  "Nor I'll none of it have;


"But now I have slain the master," he said,
  "Let me go strike the knave;
This is all the reward I ask,    205
  Nor no other will I have."


"Thou art a madman," said the sheriff;
  "Thou shouldest have had a knight's fee.

Seeing thy asking been so bad,
   Well granted it shall be."            210


But Little John heard his master speak,
   Well he knew that was his steven;
"Now shall I be loosed," quoth Little John,
   "With Christ's might in heaven."


But Robin he hied him towards Little John;  215
   He thought he would loose him belive.
The sheriff and all his company
   Fast after him did drive.


"Stand aback! stand aback!" said Robin;
   "Why draw you me so near?            220
It was never the use in our country
   One's shrift another should hear."


But Robin pulled forth an Irish knife,
   And loosed John hand and foot,
And gave him Sir Guy's bow in his hand,  225
   And bade it be his boot.


But John took Guy's bow in his hand,
   His arrows were rawstye by the root;
The sheriff saw Little John draw a bow
   And fettle him to shoot;            230


Towards his house in Nottingham
   He fled full fast away,—
And so did all his company,
   Not one behind did stay,—

But he could neither so fast go,                235
   Nor away so fast run,
But Little John with an arrow broad
   Did cleave his heart in twin.
             *Percy Fol. MS. (modernized).*


## KINMONT WILLIE

O HAVE ye na heard o' the fause Sakelde?
   O have ye na heard o' the keen Lord
     Scroope?
How they ha'e ta'en bauld Kinmont Willie,
   On Haribee to hang him up?


Had Willie had but twenty men,                5
   But twenty men as stout as he,
Fause Sakelde had never the Kinmont ta'en,
   Wi' eight score in his companie.


They band his legs beneath the steed,
   They tied his hands behind his back,                10
They guarded him, fivesome on each side,
   And they brought him o'er the Liddel-rack.


They led him through the Liddel-rack,
   And also through the Carlisle sands;
They brought him to Carlisle castle,                15
   To be at my Lord Scroope's commands.

"My hands are tied, but my tongue is free,
    And whae will dare this deed avow?
Or answer by the Border law?
    Or answer to the bauld Buccleuch?"    20


"Now haud thy tongue, thou rank reiver!
    There 's never a Scot shall set thee free:
Before ye cross my castle yate,
    I trow ye shall take farewell o' me."


"Fear na ye that, my lord," quo' Willie:    25
    "By the faith o' my body, Lord Scroope," he
        said,
"I never yet lodged in a hostelrie,
    But I paid my lawing before I gaed."


Now word is gane to the bauld keeper,
    In Branksome Ha', where that he lay,    30
That Lord Scroope has ta'en the Kinmont
        Willie,
    Between the hours of night and day.


He has ta'en the table wi' his hand,
    He gar'd the red wine spring on hie;
"Now Christ's curse on my head," he said,    35
    "But avenged of Lord Scroope I 'll be!


"O is my basnet a widow's curch?
    Or my lance a wand of the willow-tree?
Or my arm a lady's lily hand,
    That an English lord should lightly me!    40

# Kinmont Willie

"And have they ta'en him, Kinmont Willie,
  Against the truce of Border tide?
And forgotten that the bauld Buccleuch
  Is keeper here on the Scottish side?

"And have they e'en ta'en him, Kinmont
    Willie,                                     45
  Withouten either dread or fear?
And forgotten that the bauld Buccleuch
  Can back a steed, or shake a spear?

"O were there war between the lands,
  As well I wot that there is none,           50
I would slight Carlisle castle high,
  Though it were builded of marble stone.

"I would set that castle in a low,
  And sloken it with English blood!
There's never a man in Cumberland,           55
  Should ken where Carlisle castle stood.

'But since nae war's between the lands,
  And there is peace, and peace should be;
I'll neither harm English lad or lass,
  And yet the Kinmont freed shall be!"        60

He has called him forty Marchmen bauld,
  I trow they were of his ain name,
Except Sir Gilbert Elliot, called
  The Laird of Stobs, I mean the same.

He has called him forty Marchmen bauld,   65
  Were kinsmen to the bauld Buccleuch;
With spur on heel, and splent on spauld,
  And gleuves of green, and feathers blue.


There were five and five, before them a',
  Wi' hunting-horns and bugles bright;   70
And five and five came wi' Buccleuch,
  Like warden's men, arrayed for fight;


And five and five, like a mason gang,
  That carried the ladders lang and hie;
And five and five, like broken men;   75
  And so they reached the Woodhouselee.


And as we crossed the Bateable Land,
  When to the English side we held,
The first o' men that we met wi',
  Whae sould it be but fause Sakelde?   80


"Where be ye gaun, ye hunters keen?"
  Quo' fause Sakelde; "come tell to me!"
"We go to hunt an English stag,
  Has trespassed on the Scots' countrie."


"Where be ye gaun, ye marshal men?"   85
  Quo' fause Sakelde; "come tell me true!"
"We go to catch a rank reiver,
  Has broken faith wi' the bauld Buccleuch."


"Where are ye gaun, ye mason lads,
  Wi' a' your ladders, lang and hie?"   90

# Kinmont Willie

"We gang to herry a corbie's nest,
  That wons not far frae Woodhouselee."

"Where be ye gaun, ye broken men?"
  Quo' fause Sakelde; "come tell to me!"
Now Dickie of Dryhope led that band,          95
  And the never a word o' lear had he.

"Why trespass ye on the English side?
  Row-footed outlaws, stand!" quo' he.
The never a word had Dickie to say,
  Sae he thrust the lance through his fause
    bodie.                                     100

Then on we held for Carlisle toun,
  And at Staneshaw-bank the Eden we crossed;
The water was great and meikle of spait,
  But the never a horse nor man we lost.

And when we reached the Staneshaw-bank,       105
  The wind was rising loud and hie;
And there the laird gar'd leave our steeds,
  For fear that they should stamp and nie.

And when we left the Staneshaw-bank,
  The wind began full loud to blaw;           110
But 't was wind and weet, and fire and sleet,
  When we came beneath the castle wa'.

We crept on knees and held our breath,
  Till we placed the ladders against the wa';

And sae ready was Buccleuch himsel'    115
    To mount the first, before us a'.


He has ta'en the watchman by the throat,
    He flung him down upon the lead;
"Had there not been peace between our lands,
    Upon the other side thou hadst gaed!    120


"Now sound out, trumpets!" quo' Buccleuch;
    "Let 's waken Lord Scroope right merrilie!"
Then loud the warden's trumpet blew
    *O whae dare meddle wi' me?*


Then speedilie to wark we gaed,    125
    And raised the slogan ane and a',
And cut a hole through a sheet of lead,
    And so we wan to the castle ha'.


They thought King James and a' his men
    Had won the house wi' bow and spear;    130
It was but twenty Scots and ten,
    That put a thousand in sic a stear!


Wi' coulters, and wi' forehammers,
    We gar'd the bars bang merrilie,
Until we cam to the inner prison,    135
    Where Willie o' Kinmont he did lie.


And when we cam to the lower prison,
    Where Willie o' Kinmont he did lie—
"O sleep ye, wake ye, Kinmont Willie,
    Upon the morn that thou 's to die?"    140

# Kinmont Willie

"O I sleep saft and I wake aft;
   It 's lang since sleeping was fley'd frae me!
Gi'e my service back to my wife and bairns,
   And a' gude fellows that spier for me."

Then Red Rowan has hent him up,     145
   The starkest man in Teviotdale—
"Abide, abide now, Red Rowan,
   Till of my Lord Scroope I take farewell.

"Farewell, farewell, my gude Lord Scroope!
   My gude Lord Scroope, farewell!" he
      cried;     150
"I 'll pay you for my lodging maill,
   When first we meet on the Border side."

Then shoulder high, with shout and cry,
   We bore him down the ladder lang;
At every stride Red Rowan made,     155
   I wot the Kinmont's airns played clang!

"O mony a time," quo' Kinmont Willie,
   "I have ridden horse baith wild and wood;
But a rougher beast than Red Rowan
   I ween my legs have ne'er bestrode.     166

"And mony a time," quo' Kinmont Willie,
   "I 've pricked a horse out o'er the furs;
But since the day I backed a steed,
   I never wore sic cumbrous spurs!"

We scarce had won the Staneshaw-bank,   165
   When a' the Carlisle bells were rung,
And a thousand men, on horse and foot,
   Cam wi' the keen Lord Scroope along.

Buccleuch has turned to Eden Water,
   Even where it flowed frae bank to brim,   170
And he has plunged in wi' a' his band,
   And safely swam them through the stream.

He turned him on the other side,
   And at Lord Scroope his glove flung he;
"If ye like na my visit in merry England,   175
   In fair Scotland come visit me!"

All sore astonished stood Lord Scroope,
   He stood as still as rock of stane;
He scarcely dared to trew his eyes,
   When through the water they had gane.   180

"He is either himsel' a devil frae hell,
   Or else his mother a witch maun be;
I wad na have ridden that wan water
   For a' the gowd in Christentie."
                     *Scott, Minst. Scot. Bord.*

# CHEVY CHASE

## THE FIRST FIT

THE Percy out of Northumberland,
  An avow to God made he,
That he would hunt in the mountains
  Of Cheviot within days three,
In the maugre of doughty Douglas,     5
  And all that ever with him be.

The fattest harts in all Cheviot,
  He said he would kill, and carry them away:
"By my faith," said the doughty Douglas again,
  "I will let that hunting if that I may."    10

Then the Percy out of Bamborough came,
  With him a mighty meany,
With fifteen hundred archers bold, of blood and
    bone,
  They were chosen out of shires three.

This began on a Monday at morn,    15
  In Cheviot the hills so hie;
The child may rue that is unborn,
  It was the more pity.

The drivers thorough the woodes went,
  For to raise the deer;                    20
Bowmen bickered upon the bent
  With their broad arrows clear.


Then the wild thorough the woodes went,
  On every side shear;
Greyhounds thorough the greves glent       25
  For to kill their deer.


This began in Cheviot the hills aboon,
  Early on a Monenday;
By that it drew to the hour of noon,
  A hundred fat harts dead there lay.       30


They blew a mort upon the bent,
  They sembled on sides shear;
To the quarry then the Percy went,
  To see the brittling of the deer.


He said, "It was the Douglas' promise      35
  This day to meet me here;
But I wist he would fail, verament,"—
  A great oath the Percy sware.


At the last a squire of Northumberland
  Looked at his hand full nigh;            40
He was 'ware o' the doughty Douglas coming,
  With him a mighty meany;


Both with spear, bill, and brand;
  It was a mighty sight to see;

DRYBURGH ABBEY: THE GRAVE OF SCOTT

Hardier men, both of heart nor hand,    45
    Were not in Christianty.

They were twenty hundred spearmen good,
    Without any fail;
They were born along by the water o' Tweed,
    I' the bounds of Tivydale.    50

"Leave off the brittling of the deer," he said,
    "And to your bows look ye take good heed;
For never sith ye were on your mothers born
    Had ye never so mickle need."

The doughty Douglas on a steed    55
    He rode all his men beforn;
His armor glittered as did a glede;
    A bolder bairn was never born.

"Tell me whose men ye are," he says,
    "Or whose men that ye be:    60
Who gave you leave to hunt in this Cheviot
    chase,
    In the spite of mine and of me?"

The first man that ever him an answer made,
    It was the good Lord Percy:
"We will not tell thee whose men we are," he
    says,    65
    "Nor whose men that we be;
But we will hunt here in this chase,
    In the spite of thine and of thee.

"The fattest harts in all Cheviot
    We have killed and cast to carry them
      away."                       70
"By my troth," said the doughty Douglas again,
  "Therefor the ton of us shall die this day."

Then said the doughty Douglas
    Unto the Lord Percy,
"To kill all these guiltless men,        75
    Alas, it were great pity!

"But, Percy, thou art a lord of land,
    I am an earl called within my country;
Let all our men upon a party stand,
    And do the battle of thee and of me."    80

"Now Christ's curse on his crown," said the
        Lord Percy,
  "Whosoever thereto says nay!
By my troth, doughty Douglas," he says,
  "Thou shalt never see that day.

"Neither in England, Scotland, nor France,    85
    Nor for no man of a woman born,—
But, an fortune be my chance,
    I dare meet him, one man for one."

Then bespake a squire of Northumberland,
    Richard Witherington was his name;    90
"It shall never be told in South England," he
      says,
  "To King Harry the Fourth for shame.

"I wot you been great lordes twa,
   I am a poor squire of land;
I will never see my captain fight on a field,   95
   And stand myself and look on,
But while I may my weapon wield,
   I will not [fail], both heart and hand."

That day, that day, that dreadful day!
   The first fit here I find;   100
An you will hear any more o' the hunting o' the
    Cheviot
   Yet is there more behind.

### THE SECOND FIT

The Englishmen had their bows ybent,
   Their hearts were good enough;
The first of arrows that they shot off,   105
   Seven score spearmen they slough.

Yet bides the Earl Douglas upon the bent,
   A captain good enough,
And that was seen, verament,
   For he wrought hem both woe and wouch.  110

The Douglas parted his host in three,
   Like a chief chieftain of pride;
With sure spears of mighty tree,
   They come in on every side;

Through [though?] our English archery,   115
   Gave many a wound full wide;

Many a doughty they gar'd to die,
  Which gained them no pride.

The Englishmen let their bows be,
  And pulled out brands that were bright; 120
It was a heavy sight to see
  Bright swords on basnets light.

Thorough rich mail and manople [?]
  Many stern they stroke down straight;
Many a freke that was full free,            125
  There under-foot did light.

At last the Douglas and the Percy met,
  Like two captains of might and of main;
They swapped together till they both swat,
  With swords that were of fine Milan.   130

These worthy frekes for to fight,
  Thereto they were full fain,
Till the blood out of their basnets sprent,
  As ever did hail or rain.

"Yield thee, Percy," said the Douglas,      135
  "And i' faith I shall thee bring
Where thou shalt have an earl's wages
  Of Jamie our Scottish king.

"Thou shalt have thy ransom free,
  I hight thee here this thing;              140
For the manfullest man yet art thou
  That ever I conquered in field fighting."

118

# Chevy Chase

"Nay," said the Lord Percy,
  "I told it thee beforn,
That I would never yielded be          145
  To no man of a woman born."


With that there came an arrow hastily,
  Forth of a mighty wane;
It hath stricken the Earl Douglas
  In at the breast bane.                150


Thorough liver and lunges baith
  The sharp arrow is gane,
That never after in all his life-days
  He spake mo words but ane:
That was, "Fight ye, my merry men, whiles
    ye may,                            155
  For my life-days ben gane."


The Percy leaned on his brand,
  And saw the Douglas die;
He took the dead man by the hand,
  And said, "Woe is me for thee!        160


"To have saved thy life I would have parted
    with
  My lands for years three,
For a better man, of heart nor of hand,
  Was not in all the north country."


Of all that see a Scottish knight,       165
  Was called Sir Hugh the Montgomery;

He saw the Douglas to the death was dight;
　　He spended a spear, a trusty tree.

He rode upon a courser
　　Through a hundred archery,　　　　　　170
He never stinted, nor never blane,
　　Till he came to the good Lord Percy.

He set upon the Lord Percy
　　A dint that was full sore;
With a sure spear of a mighty tree　　　175
　　Clean thorough the body he the Percy bore,

O' the tother side that a man might see
　　A large cloth-yard and mair:
Two better captains were not in Christianty
　　Then that day slain were there.　　　180

An archer of Northumberland
　　Saw slain was the Lord Percy;
He bare a bend-bow in his hand,
　　Was made of trusty tree.

An arrow that a cloth-yard was lang　　185
　　To the hard steel haled he;
A dint that was both sad and sore
　　He sat on Sir Hugh the Montgomery.

The dint it was both sad and sore
　　That he of Montgomery set;　　　190
The swan-feathers that his arrow bare
　　With his heart-blood they were wet.

# Chevy Chase

There was never a freke one foot would flee,
    But still in stour did stand,
Hewing on each other, while they might
        dree,                                          195
    With many a baleful brand.


This battle began in Cheviot
    An hour before the noon,
And when even-song bell was rang,
    The battle was not half done.                      200


They took [the way?] on either hand
    By the light of the moon;
Many had no strength for to stand
    In Cheviot the hills aboon.


Of fifteen hundred archers of England       205
    Went away but seventy and three;
Of twenty hundred spearmen of Scotland,
    But even five and fifty.


But all were slain Cheviot within;
    They had no streng[th] to stand on hie;  210
The child may rue that is unborn,
    It was the more pity.


There was slain with the Lord Percy,
    Sir John of Agerstone;
Sir Roger, the hind Hartley;                           215
    Sir William, the bold Heron.

Sir George, the worthy Lumley,
  A knight of great renown,
Sir Raff, the rich Rugby,
  With dints were beaten down.      220

For Witherington my heart was woe,
  That ever he slain should be;
For when both his legs were hewn in two,
  Yet he kneeled and fought on his knee.

There was slain with the doughty Douglas,  225
  Sir Hugh the Montgomery;
Sir Davy Liddale, that worthy was,
  His sister's son was he;

Sir Charles o' Murray in that place,
  That never a foot would flee;      230
Sir Hugh Maxwell, a lord he was,
  With the Douglas did he die.

So on the morrow they made them biers
  Of birch and hazel so g[ra]y;
Many widows, with weeping tears,      235
  Came to fetch their makes away.

Tivydale may carp of care,
  Northumberland may make great moan,
For two such captains as slain were there
  On the March-party shall never be none. 240

Word is comen to Edinborough,
  To Jamie, the Scottish king,

That doughty Douglas, lieutenant of the
    Marches,
  He lay slain Cheviot within.

His hands did he weal and wring:       245
  He said, "Alas, and woe is me!"
Such another captain Scotland within,
  He said, i' faith should never be.

Word is comen to lovely London,
  Till the fourth Harry our king,      250
That Lord Percy, lieutenant of the Marches,
  He lay slain Cheviot within.

"God have mercy on his soul," said King Harry,
  "Good Lord, if Thy will it be!
I have a hundred captains in England," he
    said,      255
  "As good as ever was he:
But, Percy, an I brook my life,
  Thy death well quit shall be."

As our noble king made his avow,
  Like a noble prince of renown,      260
For the death of the Lord Percy
  He did the battle of Humbledown;

Where six-and-thirty Scottish knights
  On a day were beaten down;
Glendale glittered on their armor bright,   265
  Over castle, tower, and town.

This was the hunting of the Cheviot,
  That tear began this spurn;
Old men that knowen the ground well enough
  Call it the battle of Otterburn.    270

At Otterburn began this spurn
  Upon a Monenday;
There was the doughty Douglas slain,
  The Percy never went away.

There was never a time on the March-parties  275
  Sin the Douglas and the Percy met,
But it is marvel an the red blood run not
  As the rain does in the street.

Jesu Christ our bales bete,
  And to the bliss us bring!    280
Thus was the hunting of the Cheviot:
  God send us all good ending!

      *Child, Pop. Bal., 162A (modernized).*

## THE SKELETON IN ARMOR.

"Speak! speak! thou fearful guest!
  Who, with thy hollow breast
  Still in rude armor drest,
    Comest to daunt me!
Wrapt not in Eastern balms,
But with thy fleshless palms
Stretched, as if asking alms,
    Why dost thou haunt me?"    8

# The Skeleton in Armor

Then, from those cavernous eyes
Pale flashes seemed to rise,
As when the Northern skies
    Gleam in December;
And, like the water's flow
Under December's snow,
Came a dull voice of woe
    From the heart's chamber.                16


"I was a Viking old!
My deeds, though manifold,
No Skald in song has told,
    No Saga taught thee!
Take heed, that in thy verse
Thou dost the tale rehearse,
Else dread a dead man's curse;
    For this I sought thee.                  24


"Far in the Northern Land,
By the wild Baltic's strand,
I, with my childish hand,
    Tamed the gerfalcon;
And, with my skates fast-bound,
Skimmed the half-frozen Sound,
That the poor whimpering hound
    Trembled to walk on.                      32


"Oft to his frozen lair
Tracked I the grisly bear,
While from my path the hare
    Fled like a shadow;

Oft through the forest dark
Followed the were-wolf's bark,
Until the soaring lark
  Sang from the meadow.    40

"But when I older grew,
Joining a corsair's crew,
O'er the dark sea I flew
  With the marauders.
Wild was the life we led;
Many the souls that sped,
Many the hearts that bled,
  By our stern orders.    48

"Many a wassail-bout
Wore the long Winter out;
Often our midnight shout
  Set the cocks crowing,
As we the Berserk's tale
Measured in cups of ale,
Draining the oaken pail,
  Filled to o'erflowing.    56

"Once as I told in glee
Tales of the stormy sea,
Soft eyes did gaze on me,
  Burning yet tender;
And as the white stars shine
On the dark Norway pine,
On that dark heart of mine
  Fell their soft splendor.    64

# The Skeleton in Armor

"I wooed the blue-eyed maid,
  Yielding, yet half afraid,
  And in the forest's shade
    Our vows were plighted.
Under its loosened vest
Fluttered her little breast,
Like birds within their nest
    By the hawk frighted.    72

"Bright in her father's hall
  Shields gleamed upon the wall,
  Loud sang the minstrels all,
    Chanting his glory;
When of old Hildebrand
I asked his daughter's hand,
Mute did the minstrels stand
    To hear my story.    80

"While the brown ale he quaffed,
  Loud then the champion laughed,
  And as the wind-gusts waft
    The sea-foam brightly,
So the loud laugh of scorn,
Out of those lips unshorn,
From the deep drinking-horn
    Blew the foam lightly.    88

"She was a Prince's child.
  I but a Viking wild,
  And though she blushed and smiled,
    I was discarded!

127

Should not the dove so white
Follow the sea-mew's flight,
Why did they leave that night
    Her nest unguarded?        96


"Scarce had I put to sea,
Bearing the maid with me,
Fairest of all was she
    Among the Norsemen!
When on the white sea-strand,
Waving his armed hand,
Saw we old Hildebrand,
    With twenty horsemen.       104


"Then launched they to the blast,
Bent like a reed each mast,
Yet we were gaining fast,
    When the wind failed us;
And with a sudden flaw
Came round the gusty Skaw,
So that our foe we saw
    Laugh as he hailed us.       112


"And as to catch the gale
Round veered the flapping sail,
Death! was the helmsman's hail,
    Death without quarter!
Mid-ships with iron keel
Struck we her ribs of steel;
Down her black hulk did reel
    Through the black water!      120

# The Skeleton in Armor

" As with his wings aslant,
    Sails the fierce cormorant,
    Seeking some rocky haunt,
        With his prey laden,
    So toward the open main,
    Beating to sea again,
    Through the wild hurricane,
        Bore I the maiden.                    128


" Three weeks we westward bore,
    And when the storm was o'er,
    Cloud-like we saw the shore
        Stretching to leeward;
    There for my lady's bower
    Built I the lofty tower,
    Which, to this very hour,
        Stands looking seaward.               136


" There lived we many years;
    Time dried the maiden's tears;
    She had forgot her fears,
        She was a mother;
    Death closed her mild blue eyes,
    Under that tower she lies;
    Ne'er shall the sun arise
        On such another!                      144


" Still grew my bosom then,
    Still as a stagnant fen!
    Hateful to me were men,
        The sunlight hateful!

129

In the vast forest here,
Clad in my warlike gear,
Fell I upon my spear,
   O, death was grateful!     152


"Thus, seamed with many scars,
Bursting these prison bars,
Up to its native stars
   My soul ascended!
There from the flowing bowl
Deep drinks the warrior's soul,
*Skoal!* to the Northland! *skoal!*"
   Thus the tale ended.     160

1841.              *Henry Wadsworth Longfellow.*


# "HOW THEY BROUGHT THE GOOD NEWS FROM GHENT TO AIX"

I sprang to the stirrup, and Joris, and he;
I galloped, Dirck galloped, we galloped all
     three;
"Good speed!" cried the watch, as the gatebolts
     undrew;
"Speed!" echoed the wall to us galloping
     through;
Behind shut the postern, the lights sank to rest,
And into the midnight we galloped abreast.   6

# Good News from Ghent

Not a word to each other; we kept the great
    pace
Neck by neck, stride by stride, never changing
    our place;
I turned in my saddle and made its girths
    tight,
Then shortened each stirrup, and set the pique
    right,
Rebuckled the cheek-strap, chained slacker the
    bit,
Nor galloped less steadily Roland a whit.     12


'T was moonset at starting; but while we drew
    near
Lokeren, the cocks crew and twilight dawned
    clear;
At Boom, a great yellow star came out to see;
At Düffeld, 't was morning as plain as could be;
And from Mecheln church-steeple we heard the
    half-chime,
So Joris broke silence with, " Yet there is
    time!"               18


At Aershot, up leaped of a sudden the sun,
And against him the cattle stood black every
    one,
To stare through the mist at us galloping past,
And I saw my stout galloper Roland at last,
With resolute shoulders, each butting away
The haze, as some bluff river headland its
    spray:           24

And his low head and crest, just one sharp ear
    bent back
For my voice, and the other pricked out on his
    track;
And one eye's black intelligence,—ever that
    glance
O'er its white edge at me, his own master,
    askance!
And the thick heavy spume-flakes which aye
    and anon
His fierce lips shook upwards in gallop-
    ing on.         30


By Hasselt, Dirck groaned; and cried Joris,
    "Stay spur!
Your Roos galloped bravely, the fault's not in
    her.
We'll remember at Aix"—for one heard the
    quick wheeze
Of her chest, saw the stretched neck and stag-
    gering knees,
And sunk tail, and horrible heave of the flank,
As down on her haunches she shuddered and
    sank.         36


So, we were left galloping, Joris and I,
Past Looz and past Tongres, no cloud in the
    sky;
The broad sun above laughed a pitiless laugh,
'Neath our feet broke the brittle bright stub-
    ble like chaff;

# Good News from Ghent

Till over by Dalhem a dome-spire sprang white,
And "Gallop," gasped Joris, "for Aix is in
    sight!"          42

"How they'll greet us!"—and all in a moment
    his roan
Rolled neck and croup over, lay dead as a
    stone;
And there was my Roland to bear the whole
    weight
Of the news which alone could save Aix from
    her fate,
With his nostrils like pits full of blood to the
    brim,
And with circles of red for his eye-sockets'
    rim.          48

Then I cast loose my buffcoat, each holster let
    fall,
Shook off both my jack-boots, let go belt and
    all,
Stood up in the stirrup, leaned, patted his ear,
Called my Roland his pet-name, my horse with-
    out peer;
Clapped my hands, laughed and sang, any
    noise, bad or good,
Till at length into Aix Roland galloped and
    stood.         54

And all I remember is—friends flocking round
As I sat with his head 'twixt my knees on the
    ground;

And no voice but was praising this Roland of
    mine,
As I poured down his throat our last measure
    of wine,
Which (the burgesses voted by common con-
    sent)
Was no more than his due who brought good
    news from Ghent.        60

*1838.*   *1845.*              *Robert Browning.*


## HART–LEAP WELL

THE Knight had ridden down from Wensley
    Moor
With the slow motion of a summer's cloud,
And now, as he approached a vassal's door,
"Bring forth another horse!" he cried aloud. 4

"Another horse!"—That shout the vassal heard
And saddled his best Steed, a comely gray;
Sir Walter mounted him; he was the third
Which he had mounted on that glorious day. 8

Joy sparkled in the prancing courser's eyes;
The horse and horseman are a happy pair;
But, though Sir Walter like a falcon flies,
There is a doleful silence in the air.     12

A rout this morning left Sir Walter's Hall,
That as they galloped made the echoes roar;

# Hart-Leap Well

But horse and man are vanished, one and all;
Such race, I think, was never seen before.     16


Sir Walter, restless as a veering wind,
Calls to the few tired dogs that yet remain:
Blanch, Swift, and Music, noblest of their
    kind,
Follow, and up the weary mountain strain.     20


The Knight hallooed, he cheered and chid them
    on
With suppliant gestures and upbraidings stern;
But breath and eyesight fail; and, one by one,
The dogs are stretched among the mountain
    fern.     24


Where is the throng, the tumult of the race?
The bugles that so joyfully were blown?
—This chase it looks not like an earthly chase;
Sir Walter and the Hart are left alone.     28


The poor Hart toils along the mountain-side;
I will not stop to tell how far he fled,
Nor will I mention by what death he died;
But now the Knight beholds him lying dead.     32


Dismounting, then, he leaned against a thorn;
He had no follower, dog, nor man, nor boy:
He neither cracked his whip, nor blew his horn,
But gazed upon the spoil with silent joy.     36

Close to the thorn on which Sir Walter leaned
Stood his dumb partner in this glorious feat;
Weak as a lamb the hour that it is yeaned;
And white with foam as if with cleaving
    sleet.        40

Upon his side the Hart was lying stretched:
His nostril touched a spring beneath a hill,
And with the last deep groan his breath had
    fetched
The waters of the spring were trembling still. 44

And now, too happy for repose or rest,
(Never had living man such joyful lot!)
Sir Walter walked all round, north, south, and
    west,
And gazed and gazed upon that darling spot. 48

And climbing up the hill—(it was at least
Four roods of sheer ascent), Sir Walter found
Three several hoof-marks which the hunted
    Beast
Had left imprinted on the grassy ground.    52

Sir Walter wiped his face, and cried, "Till now
Such sight was never seen by human eyes:
Three leaps have borne him from this lofty
    brow,
Down to the very fountain where he lies.    56

"I'll build a pleasure-house upon this spot,
And a small arbour, made for rural joy;

'T will be the traveller's shed, the pilgrim's cot,
A place of love for damsels that are coy.        60


" A cunning artist will I have to frame
A basin for that fountain in the dell!
And they who do make mention of the same,
From this day forth, shall call it Hart-Leap
        Well.        64


" And, gallant stag! to make thy praises known,
Another monument shall here be raised;
Three several pillars, each a rough-hewn stone,
And planted where thy hoofs the turf have
        grazed.        68


" And in the summer-time, when days are long,
I will come hither with my paramour;
And with the dancers and the minstrel's song
We will make merry in that pleasant bower.   72


" Till the foundations of the mountains fail
My mansion with its arbour shall endure;—
The joy of them who till the fields of Swale,
And them who dwell among the woods of
        Ure!"        76


Then home he went, and left the Hart, stone-
        dead,
With breathless nostrils stretched above the
        spring.

—Soon did the Knight perform what he had
    said,
And far and wide the fame thereof did ring.  80

Ere thrice the Moon into her port had steered,
A cup of stone received the living well;
Three pillars of rude stone Sir Walter reared,
And built a house of pleasure in the dell.   84

And near the fountain, flowers of stature tall
With trailing plants and trees were inter-
    twined,—
Which soon composed a little sylvan hall,
A leafy shelter from the sun and wind.    88

And thither, when the summer days were long,
Sir Walter led his wondering paramour;
And with the dancers and the minstrel's song
Made merriment within that pleasant bower.  92

The Knight, Sir Walter, died in course of time,
And his bones lie in his paternal vale.—
But there is matter for a second rhyme,
And I to this would add another tale.    96

PART SECOND

The moving accident is not my trade;
To freeze the blood I have no ready arts:
'T is my delight, alone in summer shade,
To pipe a simple song for thinking hearts.  100

# Hart-Leap Well

As I from Hawes to Richmond did repair,
It chanced that I saw standing in a dell
Three aspens at three corners of a square;
And one, not four yards distant, near a well. 104

What this imported I could ill divine:
And, pulling now the rein my horse to stop,
I saw three pillars standing in a line,—
The last stone-pillar on a dark hill-top.        108

The trees were gray, with neither arms nor
        head;
Half wasted the square mound of tawny green;
So that you just might say, as then I said,
"Here in old time the hand of man hath
        been."                                    112

I looked upon the hill both far and near,—
More doleful place did never eye survey;
It seemed as if the spring-time came not here,
And nature here was willing to decay.            116

I stood in various thoughts and fancies lost,
When one, who was in shepherd's garb attired,
Came up the hollow:—him did I accost,
And what this place might be I then in-
        quired.                                   120

The Shepherd stopped, and that same story told
Which in my former rhyme I have rehearsed.
"A jolly place," said he, "in times of old!
But something ails it now: the spot is curst. 124

" You see these lifeless stumps of aspen wood—
  Some say that they are beeches, others elms—
  These were the bower; and here a mansion
    stood,
  The finest palace of a hundred realms!    128

" The arbour does its own condition tell;
  You see the stones, the fountain, and the stream;
  But as to the great lodge! you might as well
  Hunt half a day for a forgotten dream.    132

" There 's neither dog nor heifer, horse nor sheep,
  Will wet his lips within that cup of stone;
  And oftentimes, when all are fast asleep,
  This water doth send forth a dolorous groan.  136

" Some say that here a murder has been done,
  And blood cries out for blood: but, for my part,
  I 've guessed, when I 've been sitting in the sun,
  That it was all for that unhappy Hart.    140

" What thoughts must through the creature's
    brain have past!
  Even from the topmost stone, upon the steep,
  Are but three bounds—and look, sir, at this
    last—
  O master! it has been a cruel leap.    144

" For thirteen hours he ran a desperate race;
  And in my simple mind we cannot tell

# Hart-Leap Well

What cause the Hart might have to love this
    place,
And come and make his deathbed near the
    well.          148

" Here on the grass perhaps asleep he sank,
  Lulled by the fountain in the summer-tide;
  This water was perhaps the first he drank
  When he had wandered from his mother's
     side.        152

" In April here beneath the flowering thorn
  He heard the birds their morning carols sing;
  And he, perhaps, for aught we know, was born
  Not half a furlong from that self-same
     spring.      156

' Now, here is neither grass nor pleasant shade;
  The sun on drearier hollow never shone;
  So will it be, as I have often said,
  Till trees, and stones, and fountain, all are
     gone."      160

' Gray-headed Shepherd, thou hast spoken well;
  Small difference lies between thy creed and
    mine:
  This Beast not unobserved by Nature fell;
  His death was mourned by sympathy divine. 164

" The Being, that is in the clouds and air,
  That is in the green leaves among the groves,

Maintains a deep and reverential care
For the unoffending creatures whom he
    loves.                  168

" The pleasure-house is dust :—behind, before,
    This is no common waste, no common gloom ;
    But Nature, in due course of time, once more
    Shall here put on her beauty and her bloom. 172

" She leaves these objects to a slow decay,
    That what we are, and have been, may be
        known ;
    But at the coming of the milder day,
    These monuments shall all be overgrown.   176

" One lesson, Shepherd, let us two divide,
    Taught both by what she shows, and what
        conceals ;
    Never to blend our pleasure or our pride
    With sorrow of the meanest thing that
        feels."                180

    1800.                  *William Wordsworth.*

# THE SEA

# SIR PATRICK SPENS

THE king sits in Dunfermline town
   Drinking the blude-red wine;
" O whare will I get a skeely skipper
   To sail this new ship o' mine? "      4

O up and spak an eldern knight,
   Sat at the king's right knee:
" Sir Patrick Spens is the best sailor
   That ever sail'd the sea."      8

Our king has written a braid letter,
   And seal'd it with his hand,
And sent it to Sir Patrick Spens,   .
   Was walking on the strand.      12

" To Noroway, to Noroway,
   To Noroway o'er the faem;
The king's daughter of Noroway,
   'T is thou maun bring her hame."      16

The first word that Sir Patrick read,
   Sae loud, loud laughed he;
The neist word that Sir Patrick read
   The tear blinded his e'e.      20

# Sir Patrick Spens

"O wha is this has done this deed
    And tauld the king o' me,
To send us out, at this time of the year,
    To sail upon the sea?      24

"Be it wind, be it weet, be it hail, be it sleet,
    Our ship must sail the faem;
The king's daughter of Noroway,
    'T is we must fetch her hame."    28

They hoysed their sails on Monenday morn
    Wi' a' the speed they may;
They hae landed in Noroway
    Upon a Wodensday.    32

They hadna been a week, a week
    In Noroway but twae,
When that the lords o' Noroway
    Began aloud to say:    36

"Ye Scottishmen spend a' our king's gowd,
    And a' our queenis fee!"
"Ye lie, ye lie, ye liars loud,
    Fu' loud I hear ye lie!    40

"For I brought as much white monie
    As gane my men and me,
And I brought a half-fou o' gude red gowd
    Out o'er the sea wi' me.    44

"Mak ready, mak ready, my merry men a'!
    Our gude ship sails the morn."

"Now ever alack, my master dear,
　　I fear a deadly storm.　　　　　48

"I saw the new moon late yestreen
　　Wi' the auld moon in her arm;
And if we gang to sea, master,
　　I fear we 'll come to harm."　　52

They hadna sail'd a league, a league,
　　A league but barely three,
When the lift grew dark, and the wind
　　　blew loud,
　　And gurly grew the sea.　　　　56

The ankers brak, and the topmasts lap,
　　It was sic a deadly storm:
And the waves cam owre the broken ship
　　Till a' her sides were torn.　　60

"O where will I get a gude sailor,
　　To take my helm in hand,
Till I get up to the tall topmast,
　　To see if I can spy land?"　　64

"O here am I, a sailor gude,
　　To take the helm in hand,
Till you go up to the tall topmast;
　　But I fear you 'll ne'er spy land."　68

He hadna gane a step, a step,
　　A step but barely ane,
When a bout flew out of our goodly ship,
　　And the salt sea it came in.　　72

# Sir Patrick Spens

"Gae fetch a web o' the silken claith,
   Another o' the twine,
And wap them into our ship's side,
   And let nae the sea come in."     76


They fetch'd a web o' the silken claith,
   Another of the twine,
And they wrapp'd them round that gude
   ship's side,
   But still the sea came in.     80


O laith, laith were our gude Scots lords
   To weet their cork-heel'd shoon;
But lang or a' the play was play'd
   They wat their hats aboon.     84


And mony was the feather bed
   That flatter'd on the faem;
And mony was the gude lord's son
   That never mair cam hame.     88


The ladies wrang their fingers white,
   The maidens tore their hair,
A' for the sake of their true loves,
   For them they 'll see nae mair.     92


O lang, lang may the ladies sit,
   Wi' their fans into their hand,
Before they see Sir Patrick Spens
   Come sailing to the strand!     96

And lang, lang may the maidens sit
　　Wi' their gowd kaims in their hair,
A-waiting for their ain dear loves!
　　For them they 'll see nae mair.　　100


O forty miles off Aberdeen,
　　'T is fifty fathoms deep;
And there lies gude Sir Patrick Spens,
　　Wi' the Scots lords at his feet.　　104

*Scott, Minst. Scot. Bord.*


# ON THE LOSS OF THE ROYAL GEORGE

Toll for the brave!
　　The brave that are no more!
All sunk beneath the wave,
　　Fast by their native shore!　　4


Eight hundred of the brave,
　　Whose courage well was tried,
Had made the vessel heel,
　　And laid her on her side.　　8


A land-breeze shook the shrouds
　　And she was overset;
Down went the Royal George,
　　With all her crew complete.　　12


Toll for the brave!
　　Brave Kempenfelt is gone;

# On the Loss of the Royal George

His last sea-fight is fought,
  His work of glory done.      16

It was not in the battle;
  No tempest gave the shock;
She sprang no fatal leak,
  She ran upon no rock.      20

His sword was in its sheath,
  His fingers held the pen,
When Kempenfelt went down
  With twice four hundred men.      24

Weigh the vessel up,
  Once dreaded by our foes!
And mingle with our cup
  The tear that England owes.      28

Her timbers yet are sound,
  And she may float again
Full charged with England's thunder,
  And plough the distant main:      32

But Kempenfelt is gone,
  His victories are o'er;
And he and his eight hundred
  Shall plough the wave no more.      36

*1782.*                          *William Cowper.*

# YE MARINERS OF ENGLAND

Ye Mariners of England!
That guard our native seas;
Whose flag has braved, a thousand years,
The battle and the breeze!
Your glorious standard launch again
To match another foe!
And sweep through the deep,
While the stormy winds do blow;
While the battle rages loud and long,
And the stormy winds do blow.          10

The spirits of your fathers
Shall start from every wave!—
For the deck it was their field of fame,
And Ocean was their grave:
Where Blake and mighty Nelson fell,
Your manly hearts shall glow,
As ye sweep through the deep,
While the stormy winds do blow;
While the battle rages loud and long,
And the stormy winds do blow.          20

Britannia needs no bulwarks,
No towers along the steep;
Her march is o'er the mountain-waves,
Her home is on the deep.

With thunders from her native oak,
She quells the floods below,—
As they roar on the shore,
When the stormy winds do blow;
When the battle rages loud and long,
And the stormy winds do blow.               30

The meteor flag of England
Shall yet terrific burn;
Till danger's troubled night depart,
And the star of peace return.
Then, then, ye ocean warriors!
Our song and feast shall flow
To the fame of your name,
When the storm has ceased to blow;
When the fiery fight is heard no more,
And the storm has ceased to blow.           40

1801.                          *Thomas Campbell.*


# THE LANDING OF THE PILGRIM FATHERS IN NEW ENGLAND

THE breaking waves dashed high
    On a stern and rock-bound coast,
And the woods against a stormy sky
    Their giant branches tossed;               4

And the heavy night hung dark
    The hills and waters o'er,
When a band of exiles moored their bark
    On the wild New England shore.             8

Not as the conqueror comes,
  They, the true-hearted, came;
Not with the roll of the stirring drums,
  And the trumpet that sings of fame.        12


Not as the flying come,
  In silence and in fear,—
They shook the depths of the desert's gloom
  With their hymns of lofty cheer.         16


Amidst the storm they sang,
  And the stars heard, and the sea;
And the sounding aisles of the dim woods
    rang
  To the anthem of the free.          20


The ocean eagle soared
  From his nest by the white wave's foam,
And the rocking pines of the forest roared,—
  This was their welcome home.          24


There were men with hoary hair
  Amidst that pilgrim-band,—
Why had they come to wither there,
  Away from their childhood's land?        28


There was woman's fearless eye,
  Lit by her deep love's truth;
There was manhood's brow serenely high,
  And the fiery heart of youth.          32

What sought they thus afar?
  Bright jewels of the mine?
The wealth of seas, the spoils of war?
  —They sought a faith's pure shrine!    36

Ay, call it holy ground,
  The soil where first they trod;
They have left unstained what there they
    found,—
  Freedom to worship God.    40

**1828.**                           *Felicia Dorothea Hemans.*

## THE INCHCAPE ROCK

No stir in the air, no stir in the sea,—
The ship was as still as she could be;
Her sails from heaven received no motion;
Her keel was steady in the ocean.    4

Without either sign or sound of their shock,
The waves flowed over the Inchcape rock;
So little they rose, so little they fell,
They did not move the Inchcape bell.    8

The holy Abbot of Aberbrothok
Had placed that bell on the Inchcape rock;
On a buoy in the storm it floated and swung,
And over the waves its warning rung.    12

When the rock was hid by the surge's swell,
The mariners heard the warning bell;
And then they knew the perilous rock,
And blessed the Abbot of Aberbrothok.      16


The sun in heaven was shining gay,—
All things were joyful on that day;
The sea-birds screamed as they wheeled around,
And there was joyance in their sound.      20


The buoy of the Inchcape bell was seen,
A darker speck on the ocean green;
Sir Ralph, the rover, walked his deck,
And he fixed his eye on the darker speck.      24


He felt the cheering power of spring,—
It made him whistle, it made him sing;
His heart was mirthful to excess;
But the rover's mirth was wickedness.      28


His eye was on the bell and float:
Quoth he, "My men, put out the boat;
And row me to the Inchcape rock,
And I 'll plague the priest of Aberbrothok."  32


The boat is lowered, the boatmen row,
And to the Inchcape rock they go;
Sir Ralph bent over from the boat,
And cut the warning bell from the float.      36

# The Inchcape Rock

Down sank the bell with a gurgling sound;
The bubbles rose, and burst around.
Quoth Sir Ralph, "The next who comes to the
    rock
Will not bless the Abbot of Aberbrothok."   40

Sir Ralph, the rover, sailed away,—
He scoured the seas for many a day;
And now, grown rich with plundered store,
He steers his course to Scotland's shore.   44

So thick a haze o'erspreads the sky
They cannot see the sun on high;
The wind hath blown a gale all day;
At evening it hath died away.   48

On the deck the rover takes his stand;
So dark it is they see no land.
Quoth Sir Ralph, "It will be lighter soon,
For there is the dawn of the rising moon."   52

"Canst hear," said one, "the breakers roar?
For yonder, methinks, should be the shore.
Now where we are I cannot tell,
But I wish we could hear the Inchcape bell."   56

They hear no sound; the swell is strong;
Though the wind hath fallen, they drift along;
Till the vessel strikes with a shivering shock,—
O Christ! it is the Inchcape rock!   60

Sir Ralph, the rover, tore his hair;
He cursed himself in his despair.
The waves rush in on every side;
The ship is sinking beneath the tide.          64


But ever in his dying fear
One dreadful sound he seemed to hear,—
A sound as if with the Inchcape bell
The Devil below was ringing his knell.          68

*1801.*                                   *Robert Southey.*


# THE WRECK OF THE HESPERUS

It was the schooner Hesperus,
   That sailed the wintry sea;
And the skipper had taken his little daughter,
   To bear him company.          4


Blue were her eyes as the fairy-flax,
   Her cheeks like the dawn of day,
And her bosom white as the hawthorn buds,
   That ope in the month of May.          8


The skipper he stood beside the helm,
   His pipe was in his mouth,
And he watched how the veering flaw did
   blow
   The smoke now West, now South.          12

# The Wreck of the Hesperus

Then up and spake an old Sailòr,
    Had sailed to the Spanish Main,
"I pray thee, put into yonder port,
    For I fear a hurricane.        **16**

"Last night, the moon had a golden ring,
    And to-night no moon we see!"
The skipper, he blew a whiff from his pipe,
    And a scornful laugh laughed he.    **20**

Colder and louder blew the wind,
    A gale from t' ᵔᵔ ᵔeast,
The snow fell hissing in the brine,
    And the billows frothed like yeast.    **24**

Down came the storm, and smote amain
    The vessel in its strength;
She shuddered and paused, like a frightened
        steed,
    Then leaped her cable's length.    **28**

"Come hither! come hither! my little daughtèr,
    And do not tremble so;
For I can weather the roughest gale
    That ever wind did blow."    **32**

He wrapped her warm in his seaman's coat
    Against the stinging blast;
He cut a rope from a broken spar,
    And bound her to the mast.    **36**

"O father! I hear the church-bells ring,
　　O say, what may it be?"
"'T is a fog-bell on a rock-bound coast!"—
　　And he steered for the open sea.　　　40

"O father! I hear the sound of guns,
　　O say, what may it be?"
"Some ship in distress, that cannot live
　　In such an angry sea!"　　　44

"O father! I see a gleaming light,
　　O say, what may it be?"
But the father answered never a word,
　　A frozen corpse was he.　　　48

Lashed to the helm, all stiff and stark,
　　With his face turned to the skies,
The lantern gleamed through the gleaming
　　　snow
　　On his fixed and glassy eyes.　　　52

Then the maiden clasped her hands and
　　　prayed
　　That savèd she might be;
And she thought of Christ, who stilled the
　　　wave,
　　On the Lake of Galilee.　　　56

And fast through the midnight dark and
　　　drear,
　　Through the whistling sleet and snow,
Like a sheeted ghost, the vessel swept
　　Tow'rds the reef of Norman's Woe.　　　60

# The Wreck of the Hesperus

And ever the fitful gusts between
   A sound came from the land;
It was the sound of the trampling surf
   On the rocks and the hard sea-sand.    64


The breakers were right beneath her bows,
   She drifted a dreary wreck,
And a whooping billow swept the crew
   Like icicles from her deck.    68


She struck where the white and fleecy waves
   Looked soft as carded wool,
But the cruel rocks, they gored her side
   Like the horns of an angry bull.    72


Her rattling shrouds, all sheathed in ice,
   With the masts went by the board;
Like a vessel of glass, she stove and sank,
   Ho! ho! the breakers roared!    76


At daybreak, on the bleak sea-beach,
   A fisherman stood aghast,
To see the form of a maiden fair,
   Lashed close to a drifting mast.    80


The salt sea was frozen on her breast,
   The salt tears in her eyes;
And he saw her hair, like the brown seaweed,
   On the billows fall and rise.    84

Such was the wreck of the Hesperus,
  In the midnight and the snow!
Christ save us all from a death like this,
  On the reef of Norman's Woe!          88

*1839.*                    *Henry Wadsworth Longfellow.*


## SIR HUMPHREY GILBERT

SOUTHWARD with fleet of ice
  Sailed the corsair Death;
Wild and fast blew the blast,
  And the east-wind was his breath.      4


His lordly ships of ice
  Glisten in the sun;
On each side, like pennons wide,
  Flashing crystal streamlets run.        8


His sails of white sea-mist
  Dripped with silver rain;
But where he passed there were cast
  Leaden shadows o'er the main.          12


Eastward from Campobello
  Sir Humphrey Gilbert sailed;
Three days or more seaward he bore,
  Then, alas! the land-wind failed.       16


Alas! the land-wind failed,
  And ice-cold grew the night;

# Sir Humphrey Gilbert

And nevermore, on sea or shore,
　　Should Sir Humphrey see the light.　20

He sat upon the deck,
　　The Book was in his hand;
"Do not fear! Heaven is as near,"
　　He said, "by water as by land!"　24

In the first watch of the night,
　　Without a signal's sound,
Out of the sea, mysteriously,
　　The fleet of Death rose all around.　28

The moon and the evening star
　　Were hanging in the shrouds;
Every mast, as it passed,
　　Seemed to rake the passing clouds.　32

They grappled with their prize,
　　At midnight black and cold!
As of a rock was the shock;
　　Heavily the ground-swell rolled.　36

Southward through day and dark,
　　They drift in close embrace,
With mist and rain, o'er the open main;
　　Yet there seems no change of place.　40

Southward, forever southward,
　　They drift through dark and day;
And like a dream, in the Gulf-Stream
　　Sinking, vanish all away.　44

1848.　　　　　　　　*Henry Wadsworth Longfellow.*

# HERVÉ RIEL

On the sea and at the Hogue, sixteen hundred
    ninety-two,
  Did the English fight the French,—woe to
  France!
And, the thirty-first of May, helter-skelter
  through the blue,
Like a crowd of frightened porpoises a shoal of
  sharks pursue,
  Came crowding ship on ship to Saint Malo on
  the Rance,
With the English fleet in view.

'T was the squadron that escaped, with the
  victor in full chase;
  First and foremost of the drove, in his great
  ship, Damfreville;
Close on him fled, great and small,
Twenty-two good ships in all;
And they signalled to the place
"Help the winners of a race!
  Get us guidance, give us harbor, take us
  quick—or, quicker still,
  Here 's the English can and will!"    **14**

# Hervé Riel

Then the pilots of the place put out brisk and
     leapt on board;
"Why, what hope or chance have ships like
     these to pass?" laughed they:
"Rocks to starboard, rocks to port, all the
     passage scarred and scored,
Shall the 'Formidable' here with her twelve
     and eighty guns
     Think to make the river-mouth by the single
     narrow way,
Trust to enter where 't is ticklish for a craft of
     twenty tons,
And with flow at full beside?
Now, 't is slackest ebb of tide.
     Reach the mooring? Rather say,
While rock stands or water runs,
     Not a ship will leave the bay!"      25

Then was called a council straight.
Brief and bitter the debate:
"Here's the English at our heels; would you
     have them take in tow
All that's left us of the fleet, linked together
     stern and bow,
For a prize to Plymouth Sound?
Better run the ships aground!"
     (Ended Damfreville his speech).
"Not a minute more to wait!
     Let the Captains all and each
     Shove ashore, then blow up, burn the vessels
     on the beach!
France must undergo her fate.      36

"Give the word!" But no such word
  Was ever spoke or heard;
For up stood, for out stepped, for in struck
    amid all these
—A Captain? A Lieutenant? A Mate—first,
    second, third?
  No such man of mark, and meet
  With his betters to compete!
  But a simple Breton sailor pressed by Tour-
    ville for the fleet,
A poor coasting-pilot he, Hervé Riel the
    Croisickese.
                        44


And "What mockery or malice have we here?"
    cries Hervé Riel:
"Are you mad, you Malouins? Are you
    cowards, fools, or rogues?
Talk to me of rocks and shoals, me who took
    the soundings, tell
On my fingers every bank, every shallow, every
    swell,
  'Twixt the offing here and Grève where the
    river disembogues?
Are you bought by English gold? Is it love
    the lying's for?
Morn and eve, night and day,
Have I piloted your bay,
Entered free and anchored fast at the foot of
    Solidor.
  Burn the fleet and ruin France? That were
    worse than fifty Hogues!

# Hervé Riel

Sirs, they know I speak the truth! Sirs, be-
    lieve me there's a way!
Only let me lead the line,
  Have the biggest ship to steer,
  Get this 'Formidable' clear,
Make the others follow mine,
And I lead them, most and least, by a passage
    I know well,
  Right to Solidor past Grève,
And there lay them safe and sound;
  And if one ship misbehave,
—Keel so much as grate the ground,
Why I've nothing but my life,—here's my
    head!" cries Hervé Riel.     65

Not a minute more to wait.
"Steer us in, then, small and great!
  Take the helm, lead the line, save the
    squadron!" cried its chief.
Captains, give the sailor place!
  He is Admiral, in brief.
Still the north-wind, by God's grace!
See the noble fellow's face
As the big ship, with a bound,
Clears the entry like a hound,
Keeps the passage as its inch of way were the
    wide sea's profound!
  See, safe through shoal and rock,
  How they follow in a flock,
Not a ship that misbehaves, not a keel that
    grates the ground,
  Not a spar that comes to grief!

The peril, see, is past,
All are harbored to the last,
And just as Hervé Riel hollas "Anchor!"—
    sure as fate,
Up the English come—too late!     83

So, the storm subsides to calm:
  They see the green trees wave
  On the heights o'erlooking Grève.
Hearts that bled are stanched with balm.
"Just our rapture to enhance,
  Let the English rake the bay,
Gnash their teeth and glare askance
  As they cannonade away!
'Neath rampired Solidor pleasant riding on the
    Rance!"
How hope succeeds despair on each Captain's
    countenance!
Out burst all with one accord,
  "This is Paradise for Hell!
Let France, let France's King
Thank the man that did the thing!"
What a shout, and all one word,
  "Hervé Riel!"
As he stepped in front once more,
  Not a symptom of surprise
  In the frank blue Breton eyes,
Just the same man as before.     103

Then said Damfreville, "My friend,
I must speak out at the end,
  Though I find the speaking hard.

# Hervé Riel

Praise is deeper than the lips:
You have saved the King his ships,
  You must name your own reward.
'Faith, our sun was near eclipse!
Demand whate'er you will,
France remains your debtor still.
Ask to heart's content and have! or my name's
      not Damfreville." 113


Then a beam of fun outbroke
On the bearded mouth that spoke,
As the honest heart laughed through
Those frank eyes of Breton blue:
" Since I needs must say my say,
    Since on board the duty's done,
      And from Malo Roads to Croisic Point, what
      is it but a run?—
Since 't is ask and have, I may—
    Since the others go ashore—
Come! A good whole holiday!
    Leave to go and see my wife, whom I call the
      Belle Aurore!"
    That he asked and that he got,—nothing
      more. 125


Name and deed alike are lost:
Not a pillar nor a post
  In his Croisic keeps alive the feat as it befell;
Not a head in white and black
On a single fishing-smack.

167

In memory of the man but for whom had gone
    to wrack
      All that France saved from the fight whence
      England bore the bell.
Go to Paris: rank on rank
    Search the heroes flung pell-mell
On the Louvre, face and flank!
      You shall look long enough ere you come to
      Hervé Riel.
So, for better and for worse,
Hervé Riel, accept my verse!
In my verse, Hervé Riel, do thou once more
Save the squadron, honor France, love thy wife,
    the Belle Aurore!           140

1871.                       *Robert Browning.*

WAR

# THE BATTLE OF OTTERBURN

It fell about the Lammas tide,
  When the muir-men win their hay,
The doughty Douglas bound him to ride
  Into England, to drive a prey.

He chose the Gordons and the Graemes,     5
  With them the Lindesays, light and gay;
But the Jardines wald not with him ride,
  And they rue it to this day.

And he has burned the dales of Tyne,
  And part of Bamb'rough shire;     10
And three good towers on Reidswire fells,
  He left them all on fire.

And he marched up to Newcastle,
  And rode it round about;
"O wha's the lord of this castle,     15
  Or wha's the lady o't?"

But up spake proud Lord Percy, then,
  And O but he spake hie!
"I am the lord of this castle,
  My wife's the lady gay."     20

"If thou 'rt the lord of this castle,
 Sae weel it pleases me!
For, ere I cross the Border fells,
 The tane of us shall die."

He took a lang spear in his hand,   25
 Shod with the metal free,
And for to meet the Douglas there,
 He rode right furiouslie.

But O how pale his lady looked,
 Frae aff the castle wa',   30
When down before the Scottish spear
 She saw proud Percy fa'.

"Had we twa been upon the green,
 And never an eye to see,
I wad hae had you, flesh and fell;   35
 But your sword sall gae wi' me."

"But gae ye up to Otterburn,
 And wait there dayis three;
And if I come not ere three dayis end,
 A fause knight ca' ye me."   40

"The Otterburn 's a bonny burn;
 'T is pleasant there to be;
But there is nought at Otterburn,
 To feed my men and me.

"The deer rins wild on hill and dale,   45
 The birds fly wild from tree to tree;

# The Battle of Otterburn

But there is neither bread nor kale,
　　To fend my men and me.

" Yet I will stay at Otterburn,
　　Where you shall welcome be;　　　　　　50
And, if ye come not at three dayis end,
　　A fause lord I 'll ca' thee."

" Thither will I come," proud Percy said,
　　" By the might of Our Ladie! "
" There will I bide thee," said the Douglas,　　55
　　" My trowth I plight to thee."

They lighted high on Otterburn
　　Upon the bent sae brown;
They lighted high on Otterburn,
　　And threw their pallions down.　　　　　60

And he that had a bonny boy,
　　Sent out his horse to grass;
And he that had not a bonny boy,
　　His ain servant he was.

But up then spake a little page,　　　　　65
　　Before the peep of dawn:
" O waken ye, waken ye, my good lord,
　　For Percy 's hard at hand."

" Ye lie, ye lie, ye liar loud!
　　Sae loud I hear ye lie:　　　　　　　70
For Percy had not men yestreen
　　To dight my men and me.

"But I hae dreamed a dreary dream,
    Beyond the Isle of Sky;
I saw a dead man win a fight,          75
    And I think that man was I."

He belted on his guid braid sword,
    And to the field he ran;
But he forgot the helmet good,
    That should have kept his brain.      80

When Percy wi' the Douglas met,
    I wat he was fu' fain!
They swakked their swords, till sair they swat,
    And the blood ran down like rain.

But Percy with his guid braid sword,     85
    That could so sharply wound,
Has wounded Douglas on the brow,
    Till he fell to the ground.

Then he called on his little foot-page,
    And said, "Run speedily,       90
And fetch my ain dear sister's son,
    Sir Hugh Montgomery.

"My nephew good," the Douglas said,
    "What recks the death of ane!
Last night I dreamed a dreary dream,     95
    And I ken the day's thy ain.

"My wound is deep; I fain would sleep;
    Take thou the vanguard of the three,

And hide me by the braken bush,
　　That grows on yonder lily lee.　　100

'O bury me by the braken bush,
　　Beneath the blooming brier,
Let never living mortal ken,
　　That ere a kindly Scot lies here."

He lifted up that noble lord,　　105
　　Wi' the saut tear in his e'e;
He hid him in the braken bush,
　　That his merry men might not see.

The moon was clear, the day drew near,
　　The spears in flinders flew,　　110
But mony a gallant Englishman
　　Ere day the Scotsmen slew.

The Gordons good, in English blood,
　　They steeped their hose and shoon;
The Lindesays flew like fire about,　　115
　　Till all the fray was done.

The Percy and Montgomery met;
　　That either of other were fain;
They swapped swords, and they twa swat,
　　And aye the blood ran down between.　　120

"Yield thee, O yield thee, Percy," he said,
　"Or else I vow I'll lay thee low!"
'Whom to shall I yield," said Earl Percy,
　"Now that I see it must be so?"

**175**

"Thou shalt not yield to lord nor loun,     125
    Nor yet shalt thou yield to me;
But yield thee to the braken bush,
    That grows upon yon lily lee!"

"I will not yield to a braken bush,
    Nor yet will I yield to a brier;     130
But I would yield to Earl Douglas,
    Or Sir Hugh the Montgomery, if he were
        here."

As soon as he knew it was Montgomery,
    He struck his sword's point in the grond;
The Montgomery was a courteous knight,  135
    And quickly took him by the hond.

This deed was done at Otterburn
    About the breaking of the day;
Earl Douglas was buried at the braken bush,
    And the Percy led captive away.     140

                        *Scott, Minst. Scot. Bord.*


# AGINCOURT

*To the Cambro-Britains and
their Harp, his Ballad
of Agincourt*

FAIR stood the wind for France
    When we our sails advance,
    Nor now to prove our chance
        Longer will tarry;

176

# Agincourt

But putting to the main,
At Caux, the mouth of Seine,
With all his martial train
    Landed King Harry:      8

And taking many a fort
Furnish'd in warlike sort,
Marcheth tow'rds Agincourt
    In happy hour;
Skirmishing day by day
With those that stopp'd his way,
Where the French gen'ral lay
    With all his power.      16

Which, in his height of pride,
King Henry to deride,
His ransom to provide
    Unto him sending;
Which he neglects the while
As from a nation vile,
Yet with an angry smile
    Their fall portending.      24

And turning to his men,
Quoth our brave Henry then:
" Though they to one be ten,
    Be not amazed:
Yet have we well begun;
Battles so bravely won
Have ever to the sun
    By fame been raised.      32

177

"And for myself (quoth he)
This my full rest shall be,
England ne'er mourn for me
    Nor more esteem me:
Victor I will remain
Or on this earth lie slain,
Never shall she sustain
    Loss to redeem me.        40

"Poitiers and Cressy tell,
When most their pride did swell,
Under our swords they fell:
    No less our skill is
Than when our grandsire great,
Claiming the regal seat,
By many a warlike feat
    Lopp'd the French lilies."      48

The Duke of York so dread
The eager vaward led;
With the main Henry sped
    Among his hench-men.
Excester had the rear,
A braver man not there,—
O Lord, how hot they were
    On the false Frenchmen!      56

They now to fight are gone,
Armour on armour shone,
Drum now to drum did groan,—
    To hear was wonder.

That with the cries they make
The very earth did shake;
Trumpet to trumpet spake,
    Thunder to thunder.       64

Well it thine age became,
O noble Erpingham,
Which didst the signal aim
    To our hid forces;
When from a meadow by,
Like a storm suddenly
The English archery
    Stuck the French horses,       72

With Spanish yew so strong,
Arrows a cloth-yard long
That like to serpents stung,
    Piercing the weather;
None from his fellow starts,
But playing manly parts,
And like true English hearts,
    Stuck close together.       80

When down their bows they threw,
And forth their bilbos drew,
And on the French they flew,
    Not one was tardy;
Arms were from shoulders sent,
Scalps to the teeth were rent,
Down the French peasants went,
    Our men were hardy.       88

This while our noble king,
His broad sword brandishing,
Down the French host did ding,
    As to o'er-whelm it;
And many a deep wound lent,
His arms with blood besprent,
And many a cruel dent
    Bruised his helmet.                    96


Gloster, that duke so good,
Next of the royal blood,
For famous England stood
    With his brave brother;
Clarence, in steel so bright,
Though but a maiden knight,
Yet in that furious fight
    Scarce such another.                  104


Warwick in blood did wade,
Oxford the foe invade,
And cruel slaughter made
    Still as they ran up:
Suffolk his axe did ply,
Beaumont and Willoughby
Bare them right doughtily,
    Ferrers and Fanhope.                  112


Upon Saint Crispin's Day
Fought was this noble fray,
Which fame did not delay
    To England to carry:

## Boadicea

O when shall English men
With such acts fill a pen,
Or England breed again
    Such a King Harry!                120

1605.                    *Michael Drayton.*


## BOADICEA

WHEN the British warrior queen,
    Bleeding from the Roman rods,
Sought, with an indignant mien,
    Counsel of her country's gods,        4

Sage beneath the spreading oak
    Sat the Druid, hoary chief;
Every burning word he spoke
    Full of rage and full of grief:        8

"Princess! if our aged eyes
    Weep upon thy matchless wrongs,
'T is because resentment ties
    All the terrors of our tongues.        12

"Rome shall perish,—write that word
    In the blood that she has spilt;
Perish, hopeless and abhorred,
    Deep in ruin as in guilt.            16

"Rome, for empire far renowned,
    Tramples on a thousand states;
Soon her pride shall kiss the ground,—
    Hark! the Gaul is at her gates!        20

"Other Romans shall arise,
　　Heedless of a soldier's name;
Sounds, not arms, shall win the prize,
　　Harmony the path to fame.　　　24

"Then the progeny that springs
　　From the forests of our land,
Armed with thunder, clad with wings,
　　Shall a wider world command.　　　28

"Regions Cæsar never knew
　　Thy posterity shall sway,
Where his eagles never flew,
　　None invincible as they."　　　32

Such the bard's prophetic words,
　　Pregnant with celestial fire,
Bending as he swept the chords
　　Of his sweet but awful lyre.　　　36

She, with all a monarch's pride,
　　Felt them in her bosom glow;
Rushed to battle, fought and died,—
　　Dying, hurled them at the foe.　　　40

Ruffians, pitiless as proud,
　　Heaven awards the vengeance due;
Empire is on us bestowed,
　　Shame and ruin wait for you!　　　44

1782.　　　　　　　　　　　*William Cowper.*

# BONNY DUNDEE

To the Lords of Convention 't was Claver'se
    who spoke,
"Ere the King's crown shall fall there are crowns
    to be broke;
So let each Cavalier who loves honour and me,
Come follow the bonnet of Bonny Dundee.    4
    Come fill up my cup, come fill up my can,
    Come saddle your horses and call up your
        men;
    Come open the West Port and let me gang
        free,
    And it's room for the bonnets of Bonny
        Dundee!"    8

Dundee he is mounted, he rides up the street,
The bells are rung backward, the drums they
    are beat;
But the Provost, douce man, said, "Just e'en
    let him be,
The Gude Town is weel quit of that Deil of
    Dundee."    12

As he rode down the sanctified bends of the
    Bow,
Ilk carline was flyting and shaking her pow;

But the young plants of grace they looked
    couthie and slee,
Thinking, luck to thy bonnet, thou Bonny
    Dundee!    16

With sour-featured Whigs the Grassmarket
    was crammed,
As if half the West had set tryst to be hanged;
There was spite in each look, there was fear
    in each e'e,
As they watched for the bonnets of Bonny
    Dundee.    20

These cowls of Kilmarnock had spits and had
    spears,
And lang-hafted gullies to kill Cavaliers;
But they shrunk to close-heads and the cause·
    way was free,
At the toss of the bonnet of Bonny Dundee.    24

He spurred to the foot of the proud Castle rock,
And with the gay Gordon he gallantly spoke;
"Let Mons Meg and her marrows speak twa
    words or three,
For the love of the bonnet of Bonny Dundee."  28

The Gordon demands of him which way he
    goes—
"Where'er shall direct me the shade of Mon-
    trose!
Your Grace in short space shall hear tidings
    of me,
Or that low lies the bonnet of Bonny Dundee.  32

# Bonny Dundee

" There are hills beyond Pentland and lands be-
    yond Forth,
  If there 's lords in the Lowlands, there 's chiefs
    in the North;
  There are wild Dunie wassals three thousand
    times three,
  Will cry *hoigh!* for the bonnet of Bonny
    Dundee.            36

" There 's brass on the target of barkened bull-
    hide;
  There 's steel in the scabbard that dangles be-
    side;
  The brass shall be burnished, the steel shall
    flash free,
  At a toss of the bonnet of Bonny Dundee.    40

" Away to the hills, to the caves, to the rocks—
  Ere I own an usurper, I 'll couch with the fox;
  And tremble, false Whigs, in the midst of your
    glee,
  You have not seen the last of my bonnet and
    me! "            44

He waved his proud hand and the trumpets
    were blown,
The kettle-drums clashed, and the horsemen
    rode on,
Till on Ravelston's cliffs and on Clermiston's
    lee
Died away the wild war-notes of Bonny Dun-
    dee.            48

Come fill up my cup, come fill up my can,
Come saddle the horses and call up the
    men;
Come open your gates and let me gae free,
For it's up with the bonnets of Bonny
    Dundee!                                    52

1825.  1830.                        *Sir Walter Scott.*


# THE SOLDIER'S DREAM

OUR bugles sang truce,—for the night-cloud
    had lowered,
  And the sentinel stars set their watch in the
    sky;
And thousands had sunk on the ground over-
    powered,
  The weary to sleep, and the wounded to
    die.                                        4


When reposing that night on my pallet of straw,
  By the wolf-scaring fagot that guarded the
    slain;
At the dead of the night a sweet vision I saw,
  And thrice ere the morning I dreamt it
    again.                                      8


Methought from the battle-field's dreadful
    array,
  Far, far I had roamed on a desolate track:

# The Soldier's Dream

'T was autumn,—and sunshine arose on the
    way
  To the home of my fathers, that welcomed
    me back.           12

I flew to the pleasant fields traversed so oft
  In life's morning march, when my bosom was
    young;
I heard my own mountain-goats bleating aloft,
  And knew the sweet strain that the corn-
    reapers sung.         16

Then pledged we the wine-cup, and fondly I
    swore,
  From my home and my weeping friends never
    to part;
My little ones kissed me a thousand times o'er,
  And my wife sobbed aloud in her fulness of
    heart.          20

"Stay, stay with us,—rest, thou art weary and
    worn!"
  And fain was their war-broken soldier to
    stay;
But sorrow return'd with the dawning of morn,
  And the voice in my dreaming ear melted
    away.         24

*1800.*                       *Thomas Campbell.*

# HOHENLINDEN

On Linden, when the sun was low,
All bloodless lay the untrodden snow;
And dark as winter was the flow
    Of Iser, rolling rapidly.     4

But Linden saw another sight,
When the drum beat, at dead of night,
Commanding fires of death to light
    The darkness of her scenery.     8

By torch and trumpet fast array'd
Each horseman drew his battle-blade,
And furious every charger neigh'd
    To join the dreadful revelry.

Then shook the hills with thunder riven;
Then rush'd the steed, to battle driven;
And louder than the bolts of Heaven,
    Far flash'd the red artillery.     16

But redder yet that light shall glow
On Linden's hills of stained snow,
And bloodier yet the torrent flow
    Of Iser, rolling rapidly.     20

## The Battle of the Baltic

'T is morn, but scarce yon level sun
Can pierce the war-clouds, rolling dun,
Where furious Frank, and fiery Hun,
    Shout in their sulph'rous canopy.     24

The combat deepens. On, ye brave,
Who rush to glory, or the grave!
Wave, Munich! all thy banners wave,
    And charge with all thy chivalry!     28

Few, few shall part, where many meet!
The snow shall be their winding sheet,
And every turf beneath their feet
    Shall be a soldier's sepulchre.     32

*1800.*                 *Thomas Campbell.*

# THE BATTLE OF THE BALTIC

Of Nelson and the North,
Sing the glorious day's renown,
When to battle fierce came forth
All the might of Denmark's crown,
And her arms along the deep proudly shone;
By each gun the lighted brand,
In a bold determined hand,
And the Prince of all the land
Led them on.—          9

Like leviathans afloat,
Lay their bulwarks on the brine;
While the sign of battle flew
On the lofty British line:

It was ten of April morn by the chime:
As they drifted on their path,
There was silence deep as death;
And the boldest held his breath
For a time.—                                    18

But the might of England flush'd
To anticipate the scene;
And her van the fleeter rush'd
O'er the deadly space between.
"Hearts of oak!" our captains cried, when
        each gun
From its adamantine lips
Spread a death-shade round the ships,
Like the hurricane eclipse
Of the sun.                                     27

Again! again! again!
And the havoc did not slack,
Till a feeble cheer the Dane
To our cheering sent us back;—
Their shots along the deep slowly boom:—
Then ceased—and all is wail,
As they strike the shatter'd sail;
Or, in conflagration pale,
Light the gloom.                                36

Out spoke the victor then,
As he hail'd them o'er the wave:
"Ye are brothers! ye are men!
And we conquer but to save:—

## The Battle of the Baltic

So peace instead of death let us bring;
But yield, proud foe, thy fleet,
With the crews, at England's feet,
And make submission meet
To our King."—                                            41


Then Denmark bless'd our chief,
That he gave her wounds repose;
And the sounds of joy and grief
From her people wildly rose,
As Death withdrew his shades from the day.
While the sun look'd smiling bright
O'er a wide and woful sight,
Where the fires of funeral light
Died away.                                                54


Now joy, old England, raise!
For the tidings of thy might,
By the festal cities' blaze,
Whilst the wine-cup shines in light;
And yet amidst that joy and uproar,
Let us think of them that sleep
Full many a fathom deep,
By thy wild and stormy steep,
Elsinore!                                                63


Brave hearts! to Briton's pride
Once so faithful and so true,
On the deck of fame that died;
With the gallant good Riou:
Soft sigh the winds of Heaven o'er their
    grave!

While the billow mournful rolls,
And the mermaid's song condoles,
Singing glory to the souls
Of the brave!—                                    72

1809.                                    *Thomas Campbell.*


# AFTER BLENHEIM

It was a summer evening,
  Old Kaspar's work was done,
And he before his cottage door
  Was sitting in the sun,
And by him sported on the green
His little grandchild Wilhelmine.            6

She saw her brother Peterkin
  Roll something large and round,
Which he beside the rivulet
  In playing there had found;
He came to ask what he had found
That was so large, and smooth, and round. 12

Old Kaspar took it from the boy,
  Who stood expectant by;
And then the old man shook his head,
  And with a natural sigh,
"'T is some poor fellow's skull," said he,
"Who fell in the great victory.            18

"I find them in the garden,
  For there's many here about;

# After Blenheim

And often when I go to plough,
    The ploughshare turns them out !
For many thousand men," said he,
" Were slain in that great victory."     24

" Now tell us what 't was all about,"
    Young Peterkin, he cries ;
And little Wilhelmine looks up
    With wonder-waiting eyes ;
" Now tell us all about the war,
    And what they fought each other for."     30

" It was the English," Kaspar cried,
    " Who put the French to rout ;
But what they fought each other for,
    I could not well make out ;
But every body said," quoth he,
" That 't was a famous victory.     36

" My father lived at Blenheim then,
    Yon little stream hard by ;
They burnt his dwelling to the ground,
    And he was forced to fly ;
So with his wife and child he fled,
Nor had he where to rest his head.     42

" With fire and sword the country round
    Was wasted far and wide,
And many a childing mother then,
    And new-born baby died ;
But things like that, you know, must be
At every famous victory.     48

"They say it was a shocking sight
    After the field was won;
For many thousand bodies here
    Lay rotting in the sun;
But things like that, you know, must be
After a famous victory.          54

"Great praise the Duke of Marlbro' won,
    And our good Prince Eugene."
"Why 't was a very wicked thing!"
    Said little Wilhelmine.
"Nay . . nay . . my little girl," quoth he,
"It was a famous victory.          6c

"And every body praised the Duke
    Who this great fight did win."
"But what good came of it at last?"
    Quoth little Peterkin.
"Why that I cannot tell," said he,
"But 't was a famous victory."          66

1798.                          *Robert Southey.*


# IVRY

### A SONG OF THE HUGUENOTS

Now glory to the Lord of Hosts, from whom all
    glories are!
And glory to our Sovereign Liege, King Henry
    of Navarre!

# Ivry

Now let there be the merry sound of music and
    of dance,
Through thy corn-fields green, and sunny vines,
    oh pleasant land of France!
And thou, Rochelle, our own Rochelle, proud
    city of the waters,        5
Again let rapture light the eyes of all thy
    mourning daughters.
As thou wert constant in our ills, be joyous in
    our joy,
For cold, and stiff, and still are they who
    wrought thy walls annoy.
Hurrah! hurrah! a single field hath turned the
    chance of war,
Hurrah! hurrah! for Ivry, and Henry of
    Navarre.        10


Oh! how our hearts were beating, when, at the
    dawn of day,
We saw the army of the League drawn out in
    long array;
With all its priest-led citizens, and all its rebel
    peers,
And Appenzel's stout infantry, and Egmont's
    Flemish spears.
There rode the brood of false Lorraine, the
    curses of our land;        15
And dark Mayenne was in the midst, a trun-
    cheon in his hand:
And, as we looked on them, we thought of
    Seine's empurpled flood,

And good Coligni's hoary hair all dabbled with
    his blood;
And we cried unto the living God, who rules
    the fate of war,
To fight for His own holy name, and Henry of
    Navarre.     20

The King is come to marshal us, in all his ar-
    mour drest,
And he has bound a snow-white plume upon his
    gallant crest.
He looked upon his people, and a tear was in
    his eye;
He looked upon the traitors, and his glance was
    stern and high.
Right graciously he smiled on us, as rolled from
    wing to wing,    25
Down all our line, a deafening shout, "God save
    our Lord the King!"
"And if my standard-bearer fall, as fall full well
    he may,
For never saw I promise yet of such a bloody
    fray,
Press where ye see my white plume shine,
    amidst the ranks of war,
And be your oriflamme to-day the helmet of
    Navarre."    30

Hurrah! the foes are moving. Hark to the
    mingled din
Of fife, and steed, and trump, and drum, and
    roaring culverin.

# Ivry

The fiery Duke is pricking fast across Saint
    André's plain,
With all the hireling chivalry of Guelders and
    Almayne.
Now by the lips of those ye love, fair gentle-
    men of France,                                    35
Charge for the golden lilies,—upon them with
    the lance.
A thousand spurs are striking deep, a thou-
    sand spears in rest,
A thousand knights are pressing close behind
    the snow-white crest;
And in they burst, and on they rushed, while
    like a guiding star
Amidst the thickest carnage blazed the helmet
    of Navarre.                                        40


Now, God be praised, the day is ours.  May-
    enne hath turned his rein.
D'Aumale hath cried for quarter.  The Flemish
    count is slain.
Their ranks are breaking like thin clouds before
    a Biscay gale;
The field is heaped with bleeding steeds, and
    flags, and cloven mail.
And then we thought on vengeance, and, all
    along our van,                                     45
"Remember Saint Bartholomew," was passed
    from man to man.


But out spake gentle Henry, "No Frenchman
    is my foe:

Down, down with every foreigner, but let your
    brethren go."
Oh! was there ever such a knight, in friendship
    or in war,
As our Sovereign Lord, King Henry, the sol-
    dier of Navarre?      50

Right well fought all the Frenchmen who
    fought for France to-day;
And many a lordly banner God gave them for
    a prey.
But we of the religion have borne us best in
    fight;
And the good Lord of Rosny has ta'en the
    cornet white.
Our own true Maximilian the cornet white hath
    ta'en,      55
The cornet white, with crosses black, the flag
    of false Lorraine.
Up with it high; unfurl it wide; that all the
    host may know
How God hath humbled the proud house which
    wrought His church such woe.
Then on the ground, while trumpets sound their
    loudest point of war,
Fling the red shreds, a footcloth meet for Henry
    of Navarre.      60

Ho! maidens of Vienna; ho! matrons of Lu-
    cerne;
Weep, weep, and rend your hair for those who
    never shall return.

# Song of Marion's Men

Ho! Philip, send, for charity, thy Mexican
    pistoles,
That Antwerp monks may sing a mass for thy
    poor spearmen's souls.
Ho! gallant nobles of the League, look that
    your arms be bright;         65
Ho! burghers of Saint Genevieve, keep watch
    and ward to-night.
For our God hath crushed the tyrant, our God
    hath raised the slave,
And mocked the counsel of the wise, and the
    valour of the brave.
Then glory to His holy name, from whom all
    glories are;
And glory to our Sovereign Lord, King Henry
    of Navarre.         70

1824.                       *Lord Macaulay.*

# SONG OF MARION'S MEN

Our band is few but true and tried,
    Our leader frank and bold;
The British soldier trembles
    When Marion's name is told.
Our fortress is the good greenwood,
    Our tent the cypress-tree;
We know the forest round us,
    As seamen know the sea.

We know its walls of thorny vines,
  Its glades of reedy grass,
Its safe and silent islands
  Within the dark morass.     12


Wo to the English soldiery
  That little dread us near!
On them shall light at midnight
  A strange and sudden fear:
When, waking to their tents on fire,
  They grasp their arms in vain,
And they who stand to face us
  Are beat to earth again;
And they who fly in terror deem
  A mighty host behind,
And hear the tramp of thousands
  Upon the hollow wind.     24


Then sweet the hour that brings release
  From danger and from toil:
We talk the battle over,
  And share the battle's spoil.
The woodland rings with laugh and shout,
  As if a hunt were up,
And woodland flowers are gathered
  To crown the soldier's cup.
With merry songs we mock the wind
  That in the pine-top grieves,
And slumber long and sweetly
  On beds of oaken leaves.     36

# Song of Marion's Men

Well knows the fair and friendly moon
  The band that Marion leads—
The glitter of their rifles,
  The scampering of their steeds.
'T is life to guide the fiery barb
  Across the moonlight plain;
'T is life to feel the night-wind
  That lifts his tossing mane.
A moment in the British camp—
  A moment—and away
Back to the pathless forest,
  Before the peep of day.       48

Grave men there are by broad Santee,
  Grave men with hoary hairs;
Their hearts are all with Marion,
  For Marion are their prayers.
And lovely ladies greet our band
  With kindliest welcoming,
With smiles like those of summer,
  And tears like those of spring.
For them we wear these trusty arms,
  And lay them down no more
Till we have driven the Briton,
  For ever, from our shore.       60

1831.                       *William Cullen Bryant.*

# A BALLAD OF THE FRENCH FLEET

## OCTOBER, 1746

A FLEET with flags arrayed
  Sailed from the port of Brest,
And the Admiral's ship displayed
  The signal: "Steer southwest."
For this Admiral D'Anville
  Had sworn by cross and crown
To ravage with fire and steel
  Our helpless Boston Town.      8

There were rumors in the street,
  In the houses there was fear
Of the coming of the fleet,
  And the danger hovering near.
And while from mouth to mouth
  Spread the tidings of dismay,
I stood in the Old South,
  Saying humbly: "Let us pray!      16

"O Lord! we would not advise;
  But if in thy Providence
A tempest should arise
  To drive the French Fleet hence,

202

# A Ballad of the French Fleet

And scatter it far and wide,
  Or sink it in the sea,
We should be satisfied,
  And thine the glory be."          24


This was the prayer I made,
  For my soul was all on flame,
And even as I prayed
  The answering tempest came;
It came with a mighty power,
  Shaking the windows and walls,
And tolling the bell in the tower,
  As it tolls at funerals.          32


The lightning suddenly
  Unsheathed its flaming sword,
And I cried: "Stand still, and see
  The salvation of the Lord!"
The heavens were black with cloud,
  The sea was white with hail,
And ever more fierce and loud
  Blew the October gale.          40


The fleet it overtook,
  And the broad sails in the van
Like the tents of Cushan shook,
  Or the curtains of Midian.
Down on the reeling decks
  Crashed the o'erwhelming seas;
Ah, never were there wrecks
  So pitiful as these!          48

Like a potter's vessel broke
　　The great ships of the line;
They were carried away as a smoke,
　　Or sank like lead in the brine.
O Lord! before thy path
　　They vanished and ceased to be,
When thou didst walk in wrath
　　With thine horses through the sea!　56

1877.　　　　　　　　　　　*Henry Wadsworth Longfellow.*


## CARMEN BELLICOSUM

In their ragged regimentals,
　　Stood the old Continentals,
　　　　Yielding not,
While the grenadiers were lunging,
And like hail fell the plunging
　　　　Cannon-shot;
　　When the files
　　Of the isles,
From the smoky night encampment, bore the
　　　　banner of the rampant
　　　　Unicorn;
And grummer, grummer, grummer, rolled the
　　　　roll of the drummer
　　　　Through the morn!　　　　　11

Then with eyes to the front all,
And with guns horizontal,
　　Stood our sires;

204

# Carmen Bellicosum

While the balls whistled deadly,
And in streams flashing redly
    Blazed the fires:
    As the roar
    On the shore
Swept the strong battle-breakers o'er the green-
      sodded acres
    Of the plain;
And louder, louder, louder, cracked the black
      gunpowder,
    Cracking amain!        24


Now like smiths at their forges
Worked the red St. George's
    Cannoneers,
And the villainous saltpetre
Rang a fierce, discordant metre
    Round their ears:
    As the swift
    Storm-drift,
With hot sweeping anger, came the horseguards'
      clangor
    On our flanks.
Then higher, higher, higher, burned the old-
      fashioned fire
    Through the ranks!      36


Then the bare-headed colonel
Galloped through the white infernal
    Powder-cloud;

205

And his broad sword was swinging,
And his brazen throat was ringing
      Trumpet-loud;
      Then the blue
      Bullets flew,
And the trooper-jackets redden at the touch of
            the leaden
      Rifle-breath;
And rounder, rounder, rounder, roared the iron
            six-pounder,
      Hurling death!

1849.                          *Guy Humphreys McMaster.*


## MONTEREY

WE were not many, we who stood
  Before the iron sleet that day;
Yet many a gallant spirit would
Give half his years if but he could
  Have been with us at Monterey.          5

Now here, now there, the shot it hailed
  In deadly drifts of fiery spray,
Yet not a single soldier quailed
When wounded comrades round them wailed
  Their dying shout at Monterey.          10

And on, still on our column kept
  Through walls of flame its withering way;
Where fell the dead, the living stept,
Still charging on the guns which swept
  The slippery streets of Monterey.       15

206

# The Black Regiment

The foe himself recoiled aghast,
 When, striking where he strongest lay,
We swooped his flanking batteries past,
And braving full their murderous blast,
 Stormed home the towers of Monterey. 20

Our banners on those turrets wave,
 And there our evening bugles play;
Where orange-boughs above their grave,
Keep green the memory of the brave
 Who fought and fell at Monterey. 25

We are not many, we who pressed
 Beside the brave who fell that day;
But who of us has not confessed
He'd rather share their warrior rest
 Than not have been at Monterey? 30

*1847?*                                                    *Charles Fenno Hoffman.*


## THE BLACK REGIMENT

### MAY 27TH, 1863

Dark as the clouds of even,
Ranked in the western heaven,
Waiting the breath that lifts
All the dead mass, and drifts
Tempest and falling brand
Over a ruined land;—

207

So still and orderly,
Arm to arm, knee to knee,
Waiting the great event,
Stands the black regiment.          10


Down the long dusky line
Teeth gleam and eyeballs shine;
And the bright bayonet,
Bristling and firmly set,
Flashed with a purpose grand,
Long ere the sharp command
Of the fierce rolling drum
Told them their time had come,
Told them what work was sent
For the black regiment.          20


"Now," the flag-sergeant cried,
"Though death and hell betide,
Let the whole nation see
If we are fit to be
Free in this land; or bound
Down, like the whining hound—
Bound with red stripes of pain
In our cold chains again!"
Oh! what a shout there went
From the black regiment!          30


"Charge!" Trump and drum awoke,
Onward the bondmen broke;
Bayonet and sabre-stroke
Vainly opposed their rush,

# The Black Regiment

Through the wild battle's crush,
With but one thought aflush,
Driving their lords like chaff,
In the guns' mouths they laugh;
Or at the slippery brands
Leaping with open hands,
Down they tear man and horse,
Down in their awful course;
Trampling with bloody heel
Over the crashing steel,
All their eyes forward bent,
Rushed the black regiment.                              46

"Freedom!" their battle-cry,—
"Freedom! or leave to die!"
Ah! and they meant the word,
Not as with us 't is heard,
Not a mere party shout:
They gave their spirits out;
Trusted the end to God,
And on the gory sod
Rolled in triumphant blood.
Glad to strike one free blow,
Whether for weal or woe;
Glad to breathe one free breath,
Though on the lips of death.
Praying—alas! in vain!—
That they might fall again,
So they could once more see
That burst to liberty!
This was what "freedom" lent
To the black regiment.                                 65

209

Hundreds on hundreds fell;
But they are resting well;
Scourges and shackles strong
Never shall do them wrong.
Oh, to the living few,
Soldiers, be just and true!
Hail them as comrades tried;
Fight with them side by side;
Never, in field or tent,
Scorn the black regiment!     75

1864.                         *George Henry Boker.*


## BARBARA FRIETCHIE

Up from the meadows rich with corn,
Clear in the cool September morn,

The clustered spires of Frederick stand
Green-walled by the hills of Maryland.     4

Round about them orchards sweep,
Apple and peach tree fruited deep,

Fair as a garden of the Lord
To the eyes of the famished rebel horde,     8

On that pleasant morn of the early fall
When Lee marched over the mountain-wall;

Over the mountains winding down,
Horse and foot, into Frederick town.     12

JOHN GREENLEAF WHITTIER

# Barbara Frietchie

Forty flags with their silver stars,
Forty flags with their crimson bars,

Flapped in the morning wind: the sun
Of noon looked down, and saw not one. 16

Up rose old Barbara Frietchie then,
Bowed with her fourscore years and ten;

Bravest of all in Frederick town,
She took up the flag the men hauled down; 20

In her attic window the staff she set,
To show that one heart was loyal yet.

Up the street came the rebel tread,
Stonewall Jackson riding ahead. 24

Under his slouched hat left and right
He glanced; the old flag met his sight.

"Halt!"—the dust-brown ranks stood fast.
"Fire!"—out blazed the rifle-blast. 28

It shivered the window, pane and sash;
It rent the banner with seam and gash.

Quick, as it fell, from the broken staff
Dame Barbara snatched the silken scarf. 32

She leaned far out on the window-sill,
And shook it forth with a royal will.

"Shoot, if you must, this old gray head,
But spare your country's flag," she said.     36

A shade of sadness, a blush of shame,
Over the face of the leader came;

The nobler nature within him stirred
To life at that woman's deed and word:     40

"Who touches a hair of yon gray head
Dies like a dog! March on!" he said.

All day long through Frederick street
Sounded the tread of marching feet:     44

All day long that free flag tost
Over the heads of the rebel host.

Ever its torn folds rose and fell
On the loyal winds that loved it well;     48

And through the hill-gaps sunset light
Shone over it with a warm good-night.

Barbara Frietchie's work is o'er,
And the Rebel rides on his raids no more.  52

Honor to her! and let a tear
Fall, for her sake, on Stonewall's bier.

Over Barbara Frietchie's grave,
Flag of Freedom and Union, wave!     56

## Incident of the French Camp

Peace and order and beauty draw
Round thy symbol of light and law;

And ever the stars above look down
On thy stars below in Frederick town!  60

1863.                    *John Greenleaf Whittier.*


# INCIDENT OF THE FRENCH
# CAMP

You know, we French stormed Ratisbon:
  A mile or so away,
On a little mound, Napoleon
  Stood on our storming-day;
With neck out-thrust, you fancy how,
  Legs wide, arms locked behind,
As if to balance the prone brow,
  Oppressive with its mind.        8

Just as perhaps he mused, "My plans
  That soar, to earth may fall,
Let once my army-leader Lannes
  Waver at yonder wall,"—
Out 'twixt the battery-smokes there flew
  A rider, bound on bound
Full-galloping; nor bridle drew
  Until he reached the mound.        16

Then off there flung in smiling joy,
    And held himself erect
By just his horse's mane, a boy:
    You hardly could suspect—
(So tight he kept his lips compressed,
    Scarce any blood came through)
You looked twice ere you saw his breast
    Was all but shot in two.          24


"Well," cried he, "Emperor, by God's grace
    We've got you Ratisbon!
The marshal's in the market-place,
    And you'll be there anon
To see your flag-bird flap his vans
    Where I, to heart's desire,
Perched him!" The chief's eye flashed; his
        plans
    Soared up again like fire.          32


The chief's eye flashed; but presently
    Softened itself, as sheathes
A film the mother-eagle's eye
    When her bruised eaglet breathes;
"You're wounded!" "Nay," his soldier's
        pride
    Touched to the quick, he said:
"I'm killed, sire!" And his chief beside,
    Smiling the boy fell dead.          40

1842.                         *Robert Browning.*

# THE THREE TROOPERS

INTO the Devil tavern
  Three booted troopers strode,
From spur to feather spotted and splash'd
  With the mud of a winter road.
In each of their cups they dropp'd a crust,
  And star'd at the guests with a frown;
Then drew their swords, and roar'd for a toast,
  "God send this Crum-well-down!"       8

A blue smoke rose from their pistol locks,
  Their sword blades were still wet;
There were long red smears on their jerkins of
    buff,
  As the table they overset.
Then into their cups they stirr'd the crusts,
  And curs'd old London town;
Then wav'd their swords, and drank with a
    stamp,
  "God send this Crum-well-down!"       16

The 'prentice dropp'd his can of beer,
  The host turn'd pale as a clout;
The ruby nose of the toping squire
  Grew white at the wild men's shout.

215

Then into their cups they flung the crusts,
   And show'd their teeth with a frown;
They flash'd their swords as they gave the toast,
   "God send this Crum-well-down!"    24

The gambler dropp'd his dog's-ear'd cards,
   The waiting-women scream'd,
As the light of the fire, like stains of blood,
   On the wild men's sabres gleam'd.
Then into their cups they splash'd the crusts,
   And curs'd the fool of a town,
And leap'd on the table, and roar'd a toast,
   "God send this Crum-well-down!"    32

Till on a sudden fire-bells rang,
   And the troopers sprang to horse;
The eldest mutter'd between his teeth,
   Hot curses—deep and coarse.
In their stirrup cups they flung the crusts,
   And cried as they spurr'd through town,
With their keen swords drawn and their pis-
     tols cock'd,
   "God send this Crum-well-down!"    40

Away they dash'd through Temple Bar,
   Their red cloaks flowing free,
Their scabbards clash'd, each back-piece shone—
   None lik'd to touch the three.
The silver cups that held the crusts
   They flung to the startled town,
Shouting again, with a blaze of swords,
   "God send this Crum-well-down!"    48

1857.              *George Walter Thornbury.*

# THE CHARGE OF THE LIGHT BRIGADE

HALF a league, half a league,
  Half a league onward,
All in the valley of Death
  Rode the six hundred.
"Forward, the Light Brigade!
Charge for the guns!" he said:
Into the valley of Death
  Rode the six hundred.      8

"Forward, the Light Brigade!"
Was there a man dismayed?
Not though the soldier knew
  Some one had blundered:
Theirs not to make reply,
Theirs not to reason why,
Theirs but to do and die:
Into the valley of Death
  Rode the six hundred.      17

Cannon to right of them,
Cannon to left of them,
Cannon in front of them
  Volleyed and thundered;
Stormed at with shot and shell,
Boldly they rode and well;

Into the jaws of Death,
Into the mouth of Hell
  Rode the six hundred.     26

Flashed all their sabres bare,
Flashed as they turned in air
Sabring the gunners there,
Charging an army, while
  All the world wondered:
Plunged in the battery-smoke
Right through the line they broke:
Cossack and Russian
Reeled from the sabre-stroke,
  Shattered and sundered.
Then they rode back, but not—
  Not the six hundred.     38

Cannon to right of them,
Cannon to left of them,
Cannon behind them
  Volleyed and thundered:
Stormed at with shot and shell,
While horse and hero fell,
They that had fought so well
Came through the jaws of Death,
Back from the mouth of Hell,—
All that was left of them,
  Left of six hundred.     49

When can their glory fade?
O the wild charge they made!
  All the world wondered.

Honour the charge they made!
Honour the Light Brigade,
Noble six hundred!                              55

1854.                                    *Lord Tennyson.*

## THE CHARGE OF THE HEAVY BRIGADE AT BALACLAVA

### OCTOBER 25, 1854

THE charge of the gallant three hundred, the
   Heavy Brigade!
Down the hill, down the hill, thousands of
   Russians,
Thousands of horsemen, drew to the valley—
   and stay'd;
For Scarlett and Scarlett's three hundred were
   riding by
When the points of the Russian lances arose in
   the sky;
And he call'd "Left wheel into line!" and they
   wheel'd and obey'd.
Then he look'd at the host that had halted he
   knew not why,
And he turn'd half round, and he bade his
   trumpeter sound
To the charge, and he rode on ahead, as he
   waved his blade
To the gallant three hundred whose glory will
   never die—

219

" Follow," and up the hill, up the hill, up the hill,
Follow'd the Heavy Brigade.                    12


The trumpet, the gallop, the charge, and the
    might of the fight!
Thousands of horsemen had gather'd there on
    the height,
With a wing push'd out to the left and a
    wing to the right,
And who shall escape if they close? but he
    dashed up alone
Thro' the great gray slope of men,
Sway'd his sabre, and held his own
Like an Englishman there and then;
All in a moment follow'd with force
Three that were next in their fiery course,
Wedged themselves in between horse and horse,
Fought for their lives in the narrow gap they
    had made—
Four amid thousands! and up the hill, up the
    hill,
Gallopt the gallant three hundred, the Heavy
    Brigade.                    25


Fell like a cannonshot,
Burst like a thunderbolt,
Crash'd like a hurricane,
Broke thro' the mass from below,
Drove thro' the midst of the foe,
Plunged up and down, to and fro,
Rode flashing blow upon blow,

# The Heavy Brigade

Brave Inniskillens and Greys
Whirling their sabres in circles of light!
And some of us, all in amaze,
Who were held for a while from the fight,
And were only standing at gaze,
When the dark-muffled Russian crowd
Folded its wings from the left and the right,
And roll'd them around like a cloud,—
O mad for the charge and the battle were we,
When our own good redcoats sank from sight,
Like drops of blood in a dark-gray sea,
And we turn'd to each other, whispering, all
    dismay'd,
' Lost are the gallant three hundred of Scarlett's
    Brigade! "            45


' Lost one and all " were the words
Mutter'd in our dismay;
But they rode like Victors and Lords
Thro' the forest of lances and swords
In the heart of the Russian hordes,
They rode, or they stood at bay—
Struck with the sword-hand and slew,
Down with the bridle-hand drew
The foe from the saddle and threw
Underfoot there in the fray—
Ranged like a storm or stood like a rock
In the wave of a stormy day;
Till suddenly shock upon shock
Stagger'd the mass from without,
Drove it in wild disarray,

221

For our men gallopt up with a cheer and a
    shout,
And the foeman surged, and waver'd, and
    reel'd
Up the hill, up the hill, up the hill, out of the
    field,
And over the brow and away.         64

Glory to each and to all, and the charge that
    they made!
Glory to all the three hundred, and all the
    Brigade!         66
  1882.                     *Lord Tennyson.*

# THE REVENGE

### A BALLAD OF THE FLEET

At Flores in the Azores Sir Richard Grenville
    lay,
And a pinnace, like a flutter'd bird, came flying
    from far away;
" Spanish ships of war at sea! we have sighted
    fifty-three!"
Then sware Lord Thomas Howard: "'Fore
    God I am no coward;
But I cannot meet them here, for my ships are
    out of gear,

# The Revenge

And the half my men are sick. I must fly, but
  follow quick.
We are six ships of the line; can we fight with
  fifty-three?"                                        7


Then spake Sir Richard Grenville: "I know
  you are no coward;
You fly them for a moment to fight with them
  again.
But I 've ninety men and more that are lying
  sick ashore.
I should count myself the coward if I left them,
  my Lord Howard,
To these Inquisition dogs and the devildoms of
  Spain."                                              12


So Lord Howard past away with five ships of
  war that day,
Till he melted like a cloud in the silent summer
  heaven;
But Sir Richard bore in hand all his sick men
  from the land
Very carefully and slow,
Men of Bideford in Devon,
And we laid them on the ballast down below;
For we brought them all aboard,
And they blest him in their pain, that they were
  not left to Spain,
To the thumbscrew and the stake, for the
  glory of the Lord.                                   21

He had only a hundred seamen to work the ship
    and to fight,
And he sailed away from Flores till the
    Spaniard came in sight,
With his huge sea-castles heaving upon the
    weather bow.
"Shall we fight or shall we fly?
Good Sir Richard, tell us now,
For to fight is but to die!
There'll be little of us left by the time this sun
    be set."
And Sir Richard said again: "We be all good
    English men.
Let us bang these dogs of Seville, the children
    of the devil,
For I never turn'd my back upon Don or devil
    yet."      31

Sir Richard spoke and he laugh'd, and we
    roar'd a hurrah, and so
The little Revenge ran on sheer into the heart
    of the foe,
With her hundred fighters on deck, and her
    ninety sick below;
For half of their fleet to the right and half to
    the left were seen,
And the little Revenge ran on thro' the long
    sea-lane between.      36

Thousands of their soldiers look'd down from
    their decks and laugh'd,
Thousands of their seamen made mock at the
    mad little craft

# The Revenge

Running on and on, till delay'd
By their mountain-like San Philip that, of fif-
  teen hundred tons,
And up-shadowing high above us with her
  yawning tiers of guns,
Took the breath from our sails, and we stay'd. 42

And while now the great San Philip hung
  above us like a cloud
Whence the thunderbolt will fall
Long and loud,
Four galleons drew away
From the Spanish fleet that day,
And two upon the larboard and two upon the
  starboard lay,
And the battle-thunder broke from them all. 49

But anon the great San Philip, she bethought
  herself and went,
Having that within her womb that had left her
  ill content;
And the rest they came aboard us, and they
  fought us hand to hand,
For a dozen times they came with their pikes
  and musqueteers,
And a dozen times we shook 'em off as a dog
  that shakes his ears
When he leaps from the water to the land. 55

And the sun went down, and the stars came out
  far over the summer sea,
But never a moment ceased the fight of the one
  and the fifty-three.

Ship after ship, the whole night long, their
    high-built galleons came,
Ship, after ship, the whole night long, with her
    battle-thunder and flame;
Ship after ship, the whole night long, drew back
    with her dead and her shame.
For some were sunk and many were shatter'd,
    and so could fight us no more—
God of battles, was ever a battle like this in the
    world before?       64

For he said, "Fight on! fight on!"
Tho' his vessel was all but a wreck;
And it chanced that, when half of the short
    summer night was gone,
With a grisly wound to be drest he had left
    the deck,
But a bullet struck him that was dressing it
    suddenly dead,
And himself he was wounded again in the side
    and the head,
And he said, "Fight on! fight on!"     69

And the night went down, and the sun smiled
    out far over the summer sea,
And the Spanish fleet with broken sides lay
    round us all in a ring;
But they dared not touch us again, for they
    fear'd that we still could sting,
So they watch'd what the end would be.
And we had not fought them in vain,
But in perilous plight were we,
Seeing forty of our poor hundred were slain,

226

# The Revenge

And half of the rest of us maim'd for life
In the crash of the cannonades and the des-
    perate strife;
And the sick men down in the hold were most
    of them stark and cold,
And the pikes were all broken or bent, and the
    powder was all of it spent;
And the masts and the rigging were lying over
    the side;
But Sir Richard cried in his English pride:
"We have fought such a fight for a day and a
    night
As may never be fought again!
We have won great glory, my men!
And a day less or more
At sea or ashore,
We die—does it matter when?
Sink me the ship, Master Gunner—sink her,
    split her in twain!
Fall into the hands of God, not into the hands
    of Spain!"       90


And the gunner said, "Ay, ay," but the seamen
    made reply:
"We have children, we have wives,
And the Lord hath spared our lives.
We will make the Spaniard promise, if we
    yield, to let us go;
We shall live to fight again and to strike an-
    other blow."
And the lion there lay dying, and they yielded
    to the foe.      96

And the stately Spanish men to their flagship
    bore him then,
Where they laid him by the mast, old Sir
    Richard caught at last,
And they praised him to his face with their
    courtly foreign grace;
But he rose upon their decks, and he cried:
'I have fought for Queen and Faith like a
    valiant man and true;
I have only done my duty as a man is bound
    to do.
With a joyful spirit I Sir Richard Grenville
    die!"
And he fell upon their decks, and he died. 104


And they stared at the dead that had been so
    valiant and true,
And had holden the power and glory of Spain
    so cheap
That he dared her with one little ship and his
    English few;
Was he devil or man? He was devil for aught
    they knew,
But they sank his body with honour down into
    the deep.
And they mann'd the Revenge with a swarthier
    alien crew,
And away she sail'd with her loss and long'd
    for her own;
When a wind from the lands they had ruin'd
    awoke from sleep,

# The Revenge

And the water began to heave and the weather
    to moan,
And or ever that evening ended a great gale
    blew,
And a wave like the wave that is raised by an
    earthquake grew,
Till it smote on their hulls and their sails and
    **their masts and their flags,**
And the whole sea plunged and fell on the
    shot-shatter'd navy of Spain,
And the little Revenge herself went down by
    the island crags
To be lost evermore in the main.     119

1878.                      *Lord Tennyson.*

...go to men to marry anyone would
        most...

And so... that woman could a... they had

And ... saw the dry ... that it seemed to all
        embracing new

... Fires smote on their hulls and their sails, and
        their masts and their flags

And the whole sea glimmer and not all the
        gold-shafted ... flag of Spain

And the little dwyn...larva'd with great ...
        chesland sail

To be first seen on the ocean ...

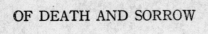

OF DEATH AND SORROW

# FAIR HELEN OF KIRCONNELL

I wish I were where Helen lies!
Night and day on me she cries;
O that I were where Helen lies,
   On fair Kirconnell Lee!

Curst be the heart that thought the
      thought,                                  5
And curst the hand that fired the shot,
When in my arms burd Helen dropt,
   And died to succour me.

O thinkna ye my heart was sair,
When my love dropt down and spak nae
      mair!                                     10
There did she swoon wi' meikle care,
   On fair Kirconnell Lee.

As I went down the water-side,
None but my foe to be my guide,
None but my foe to be my guide,                 15
   On fair Kirconnell Lee.

I lighted down, my sword did draw,
I hacked him in pieces sma',
I hacked him in pieces sma',
   For her sake that died for me.                20

233

O Helen fair, beyond compare!
I 'll make a garland of thy hair,
Shall bind my heart for evermair,
   Until the day I die.

O that I were where Helen lies!      25
Night and day on me she cries;
Out of my bed she bids me rise,
   Says, " Haste, and come to me!"—

O Helen fair! O Helen chaste!
If I were with thee, I were blest,      30
Where thou lies low, and takes thy rest,
   On fair Kirconnell Lee.

I wish my grave were growing green,
A winding-sheet drawn ower my e'en,
And I in Helen's arms lying,      35
   On fair Kirconnell Lee.

I wish I were where Helen lies!
Night and day on me she cries;
And I am weary of the skies,
   For her sake that died for me.      40

*Scott, Minst. Scot. Bord.*


# ROBIN HOOD'S DEATH

WHEN Robin Hood and Little John
   *Down a down, a down, a down*
Went o'er yon bank of broom,
  Said Robin Hood bold to Little John,

# Robin Hood's Death

" We have shot for many a pound.               5
  *Hey, down, a down, a down.*

" But I am not able to shoot one shot more,
    My broad arrows will not flee;
  But I have a cousin lives down below,
    Please God, she will bleed me."          10

  Now Robin he is to fair Kirkley gone,
    As fast as he can win;
  But before he came there, as we do hear,
    He was taken very ill.

  And when he came to fair Kirkley-hall,     15
    He knocked all at the ring,
  But none was so ready as his cousin herself
    For to let bold Robin in.

" Will you please to sit down, cousin Robin,"
        she said,
    " And drink some beer with me?"           20
" No, I will neither eat nor drink,
    Till I am blooded by thee."

" Well, I have a room, cousin Robin," she said,
    " Which you did never see,
  And if you please to walk therein,          25
    You blooded by me shall be."

  She took him by the lily-white hand,
    And led him to a private room,
  And there she blooded bold Robin Hood,
    While one drop of blood would run down. 30

She blooded him in the vein of the arm,
    And locked him up in the room;
Then did he bleed all the live-long day,
    Until the next day at noon.

He then bethought him of a casement there, 35
    Thinking for to get down;
But was so weak he could not leap,
    He could not get him down.

He then bethought him of his bugle-horn,
    Which hung low down to his knee;     40
He set his horn unto his mouth,
    And blew out weak blasts three.

Then Little John, when hearing him,
    As he sat under a tree,
"I fear my master is now near dead,     45
    He blows so wearily."

Then Little John to fair Kirkley is gone,
    As fast as he can dree;
But when he came to Kirkley-hall,
    He broke locks two or three:     50

Until he came bold Robin to see,
    Then he fell on his knee;
"A boon, a boon," cries Little John,
    "Master, I beg of thee."

"What is that boon," quoth Robin Hood,     55
    "Little John, [thou] begs of me?"

# Robin Hood's Death

"It is to burn fair Kirkley-hall,
    And all their nunnery."

"Now nay, now nay," quoth Robin Hood,
    "That boon I'll not grant thee;        60
I never hurt woman in all my life,
    Nor man in woman's company.

"I never hurt fair maid in all my time,
    Nor at mine end shall it be;
But give me my bent bow in my hand,        65
    And a broad arrow I'll let flee;
And where this arrow is taken up,
    There shall my grave digged be.

"Lay me a green sod under my head,
    And another at my feet;        70
And lay my bent bow by my side,
    Which was my music sweet;
And make my grave of gravel and green,
    Which is most right and meet.

"Let me have length and breadth enough,        75
    With a green sod under my head;
That they may say, when I am dead,
    Here lies bold Robin Hood."

These words they readily granted him,
    Which did bold Robin please:        80
And there they buried bold Robin Hood,
    Within the fair Kirkleys.

*Child, Pop. Bal., No. 120B.*

# BONNIE GEORGE CAMPBELL

Hie upon Hielands and low upon Tay,
Bonnie George Campbell rade out on a day.

Saddled and bridled and gallant rade he;
Hame cam his guid horse, but never cam he.

Out cam his auld mither greeting fu' sair,  5
And out cam his bonnie bride rivin' her hair.

Saddled and bridled and booted rade he;
Toom hame cam the saddle, but never cam he.

"My meadow lies green, and my corn is unshorn,
My barn is to big, and my **babie 's unborn**." 10

Saddled and bridled and booted rade he;
Toom hame cam the saddle, but never cam he.

*Child, No. 210 (Motherwell's Version).*


# LORD RANDAL

"O where ha'e ye been, Lord Randal, my son?
O where ha'e ye been, my handsome young
man?"

# Lord Randal

" I ha'e been to the wild wood; mother, make my
   bed soon;
   For I 'm weary wi' hunting, and fain wald lie
   down." 4

" Where gat ye your dinner, Lord Randal, my
   son?
   Where gat ye your dinner, my handsome young
   man?"
" I dined wi' my true-love; mother, make my bed
   soon;
   For I 'm weary wi' hunting, and fain wald lie
   down." 8

" What gat ye to your dinner, Lord Randal, my
   son?
   What gat ye to your dinner, my handsome
   young man?"
" I gat eels boiled in broo'; mother, make my bed
   soon;
   For I 'm weary wi' hunting, and fain wald lie
   down." 12

" What became of your bloodhounds, Lord Randal, my son?
   What became of your bloodhounds, my handsome young man?"
' O they swelled and they died; mother, make
   my bed soon;
   For I 'm weary wi' hunting, and fain wald lie
   down." 16

"O I fear ye are poisoned, Lord Randal, my son!
　O I fear ye are poisoned, my handsome young
　　man!"
"O yes! I am poisoned; mother, make my bed
　　soon;
　For I'm sick at the heart, and I fain wald lie
　　down."　　　　　　　　　　　　　　　　20

*Scott, Minst. Scot. Bord.*


## THE WIFE OF USHER'S WELL

THERE lived a wife at Usher's Well,
　And a wealthy wife was she;
She had three stout and stalwart sons,
　And sent them o'er the sea.

They hadna been a week from her,　　　　　5
　A week but barely ane,
Whan word came to the carline wife,
　That her three sons were gane.

They hadna been a week from her,
　A week but barely three,　　　　　　　10
Whan word came to the carline wife,
　That her sons she'd never see.

"I wish the wind may never cease,
　Nor fishes in the flood,
Till my three sons come hame to me,　　15
　In earthly flesh and blood!"

# The Wife of Usher's Well

It fell about the Martinmas,
  When nights are lang and mirk,
The carline wife's three sons came hame,
  And their hats were o' the birk.     20

It neither grew in syke nor ditch,
  Nor yet in ony sheugh;
But at the gates o' Paradise,
  That birk grew fair eneugh.

    *     *     *     *     *

"Blow up the fire, my maidens!     25
  Bring water from the well!
For a' my house shall feast this night,
  Since my three sons are well."

And she has made to them a bed,
  She's made it large and wide;     30
And she's ta'en her mantle her about,
  Sat down at the bed-side.

    *     *     *     *     *

Up then crew the red, red cock,
  And up and crew the gray;
The eldest to the youngest said,     35
  "'T is time we were away."

The cock he hadna crawed but once,
  And clapped his wings at a',
Whan the youngest to the eldest said,
  "Brother, we must awa'.     40

"The cock doth craw, the day doth daw',
  The channerin' worm doth chide;

Gin we be missed out o' our place,
    A sair pain we maun bide.       44

"Fare ye weel, my mother dear!
    **Fareweel** to barn and byre!
And fare ye weel, the bonny lass,
    That kindles my mother's fire."    48
    *       *       *       *       *

*Scott, Minst. Scot. Bord.*

## THE DOUGLAS TRAGEDY

"Rise up, rise up, now, Lord Douglas," she says,
    "And put on your armour so bright;
Let it never be said that a daughter of thine
    Was married to a lord under night.

"Rise up, rise up, my seven bold sons,    5
    And put on your armour so bright,
And take better care of your youngest sister,
    For your eldest's awa' the last night."

He's mounted her on a milk-white steed,
    And himself on a dapple grey,    10
With a bugelet horn hung down by his side,
    And lightly they rode away.

Lord William lookit o'er his left shoulder,
    To see what he could see,
And there he spied her seven brethren bold,    15
    Come riding o'er the lee.

# The Douglas Tragedy

"Light down, light down, Lady Marg'ret," he
    said,
  "And hold my steed in your hand,
Until that against your seven brethren bold,
    And your father, I mak a stand."    20

She held his steed in her milk-white hand,
    And never shed one tear,
Until that she saw her seven brethren fa',
    And her father hard fighting, who loved her
      so dear.

"O hold your hand, Lord William!" she said,  25
  "For your strokes they are wond'rous sair;
True lovers I can get many a ane,
    But a father I can never get mair."

O she 's ta'en out her handkerchief,
    It was o' the holland sae fine,    30
And aye she dighted her father's bloody
    wounds,
    That were redder than the wine.

"O chuse, O chuse, Lady Marg'ret," he said,
  "O whether will ye gang or bide?"
"I 'll gang, I 'll gang, Lord William," she said,  35
  "For ye have left me no other guide."

He 's lifted her on a milk-white steed,
    And himself on a dapple grey,
With a bugelet horn hung down by his side,
    And slowly they baith rade away.    40

O they rade on, and on they rade,
   And a' by the light of the moon,
Until they came to yon wan water,
   And there they lighted down.

They lighted down to tak a drink ,     45
   Of the spring that ran sae clear;
And down the stream ran his gude heart's
     blood,
   And sair she 'gan to fear.

"Hold up, hold up, Lord William," she says,
   "For I fear that you are slain!"     50
"'T is naething but the shadow of my scarlet
     cloak,
   That shines in the water sae plain."

O they rade on, and on they rade,
   And a' by the light of the moon,
Until they cam to his mother's ha' door,     55
   And there they lighted down.

"Get up, get up, lady mother," he says,
   "Get up, and let me in!
Get up, get up, lady mother!" he says,
   "For this night my fair lady I 've win.     60

"O mak my bed, lady mother," he says,
   "O mak it braid and deep!
And lay Lady Marg'ret close at my back,
   And the sounder I will sleep."

Lord William was dead lang ere midnight,   65
  Lady Marg'ret lang ere day—
And all true lovers that go thegither,
  May they have mair luck than they!

Lord William was buried in St. Mary's kirk,
  Lady Margaret in Mary's quire;   70
Out o' the lady's grave grew a bonny red rose,
  And out o' the knight's a brier.

And they twa met, and they twa plat,
  And fain they wad be near;
And a' the warld might ken right weel,   75
  They were twa lovers dear.

But bye and rade the Black Douglas,
  And wow but he was rough!
For he pulled up the bonny brier,
  **And flang 't in St. Mary's Loch.**   80

*Scott, Minst. Scot. Bord.*


# THE TWA CORBIES

As I was walking all alane,
I heard twa corbies making a mane:
The tane unto the t' other say,
"Whar sall we gang and dine to-day?"   **4**

"—In behint yon auld fail dyke
I wot there lies a new-slain knight;

245

And naebody kens that he lies there
But his hawk, his hound, and lady fair.      8

"His hound is to the hunting gane,
His hawk to fetch the wild-fowl hame,
His lady's ta'en another mate,
So we may mak our dinner sweet.      12

"Ye'll sit on his white hause-bane,
And I'll pike out his bonny blue e'en:
Wi' ae lock o' his gowden hair
"We'll theek our nest when it grows bare. 16

"Mony a one for him makes mane,
But nane sall ken whare he is gane:
O'er his white banes, when they are bare,
The wind sall blaw for evermair."      20

*Scott, Minst. Scot. Bord.*


# THE BRAES OF YARROW

LATE at een, drinkin' the wine,
   Or early in a mornin',
They set a combat them between,
   To fight it in the dawnin'.      4

"O stay at hame, my noble lord!
   O stay at hame, my marrow!
My cruel brother will you betray,
   On the dowie houms o' Yarrow."      8

# The Braes of Yarrow

"O fare ye weel, my lady gay!
 O fare ye weel, my Sarah!
For I maun gae, tho' I ne'er return
 Frae the dowie banks o' Yarrow."  12

She kiss'd his cheek, she kaimed his hair,
 As she had done before, O;
She belted on his noble brand,
 An' he's awa to Yarrow.  16

O he's gane up yon high, high hill—
 I wat he gaed wi' sorrow—
An' in a den spied nine arm'd men,
 I' the dowie houms o' Yarrow.  20

"O are ye come to drink the wine,
 As ye hae doon before, O?
Or are ye come to wield the brand,
 On the bonnie banks o' Yarrow?"  24

"I am no come to drink the wine,
 As I hae doon before, O,
But I am come to wield the brand,
 On the dowie houms o' Yarrow."  28

Four he hurt, an' five he slew,
 On the dowie houms o' Yarrow,
Till that stubborn knight came him behind,
 An' ran his body thorrow.  32

"Gae hame, gae hame, good brother John,
 An' tell your sister Sarah

To come an' lift her noble lord,
 Who's sleepin' sound on Yarrow."   36

"Yestreen I dream'd a dolefu' dream;
 I kend there wad be sorrow;
I dream'd I pu'd the heather green,
 On the dowie banks o' Yarrow."   40

She gaed up yon high, high hill—
 I wat she gaed wi' sorrow—
An' in a den spied nine dead men,
 On the dowie houms o' Yarrow.   44

She kiss'd his cheek, she kaimed his hair,
 As oft she did before, O;
She drank the red blood frae him ran,
 On the dowie houms o' Yarrow.   48

"O haud your tongue, my douchter dear,
 For what needs a' this sorrow?
I'll wed you on a better lord
 Than him you lost on Yarrow."   52

"O haud your tongue, my father dear,
 An' dinna grieve your Sarah;
A better lord was never born
 Than him I lost on Yarrow.   56

"Tak hame your ousen, tak hame your kye,
 For they hae bred our sorrow;
I wiss that they had a' gane mad
 Whan they cam first to Yarrow."   60

*Child, Pop. Bal., No. 214E.*

# THY BRAES WERE BONNY

"Thy braes were bonny, Yarrow stream,
　　When first on them I met my lover;
Thy braes how dreary, Yarrow stream,
　　When now thy waves his body cover!
For ever now, O Yarrow stream!
　　Thou art to me a stream of sorrow;
For never on thy banks shall I
　　Behold my Love, the flower of Yarrow. 8

"He promised me a milk-white steed
　　To bear me to his father's bowers;
He promised me a little page
　　To 'squire me to his father's towers;
He promised me a wedding-ring,—
　　The wedding-day was fix'd to-morrow;—
Now he is wedded to his grave,
　　Alas, his watery grave in Yarrow! 16

"Sweet were his words when last we met;
　　My passion I as freely told him;
Clasp'd in his arms, I little thought
　　That I should never more behold him!
Scarce was he gone, I saw his ghost;
　　It vanish'd with a shriek of sorrow;
Thrice did the water-wraith ascend,
　　And gave a doleful groan thro' Yarrow. 24

"His mother from the window look'd
    With all the longing of a mother;
His little sister weeping walk'd
    The green-wood path to meet her brother;
They sought him east, they sought him
        west,
    They sought him all the forest thorough;
They only saw the cloud of night,
    They only heard the roar of Yarrow.   32

"No longer from thy window look—
    Thou hast no son, thou tender mother!
No longer walk, thou lovely maid;
    Alas, thou hast no more a brother!
No longer seek him east or west,
    And search no more the forest thorough;
For, wandering in the night so dark,
    He fell a lifeless corse in Yarrow.   40

"The tear shall never leave my cheek,
    No other youth shall be my marrow—
I 'll seek thy body in the stream,
    And then with thee I 'll sleep in **Yarrow**."
—The tear did never leave her cheek,
    No other youth became her marrow;
She found his body in the stream,
    And now with him she sleeps in Yarrow.   48

1781-2.                                    *John Logan.*

250

# A LAMENT FOR FLODDEN

I 'VE heard the lilting at our ewe-milking,
    Lasses a-lilting before the dawn of day;
But now they are moaning on ilka green loaning—
    The Flowers of the Forest are a' wede away. 4

At bughts, in the morning, nae blithe lads are
    scorning,
    Lasses are lonely and dowie and wae;
Nae daffing, nae gabbing, but sighing and sab-
    bing,
    Ilk ane lifts her leglin and hies her away.     8

In hairst, at the shearing, nae youths now are
    jeering,
    Bandsters are lyart, and runkled, and gray:
At fair or at preaching, nae wooing, nae fleech-
    ing—
    The Flowers of the Forest are a' wede away. 12

At e'en, at the gloaming, nae swankies are roam-
    ing,
    'Bout stacks wi' the lasses at bogle to play;
But ilk ane sits drearie, lamenting her dearie—
    The Flowers of the Forest are a' wede away. 16

Dool and wae for the order sent our lads to the
   Border!
  The English, for ance, by guile wan the day;
The Flowers of the Forest, that fought aye the
   foremost,
  The prime o' our land, are cauld in the clay. 20

We hear nae mair lilting at our ewe-milking;
  Women and bairns are heartless and wae;
Sighing and moaning on ilka green loaning—
  The Flowers of the Forest are a' wede away. 24
*1755.*                 *Jean Elliot.*


## WE ARE SEVEN

——A SIMPLE Child,
  That lightly draws its breath,
And feels its life in every limb,
  What should it know of death?     4

I met a little cottage Girl:
  She was eight years old, she said;
Her hair was thick with many a curl
  That clustered round her head.     8

She had a rustic, woodland air,
  And she was wildly clad:
Her eyes were fair, and very fair;
  ——Her beauty made me glad.     12

# We are Seven

"Sisters and brothers, little Maid,
　　How many may you be?"
"How many? Seven in all," she said
　　And wondering looked at me.　　　　16

"And where are they? I pray you tell."
　　She answered, "Seven are we;
And two of us at Conway dwell,
　　And two are gone to sea.　　　　20

"Two of us in the church-yard lie,
　　My sister and my brother;
And in the church-yard cottage, I
　　Dwell near them with my mother."　　24

"You say that two at Conway dwell,
　　And two are gone to sea,
Yet ye are seven!—I pray you tell,
　　Sweet Maid, how this may be."　　28

Then did the little Maid reply,
　　"Seven boys and girls are we;
Two of us in the church-yard lie,
　　Beneath the church-yard tree."　　32

"You run about, my little Maid,
　　Your limbs they are alive;
If two are in the church-yard laid,
　　Then ye are only five."　　36

"Their graves are green, they may be seen,"
　　The little Maid replied,

"Twelve steps or more from my mother's
    door,
    And they are side by side.     40

"My stockings there I often knit,
    My kerchief there I hem;
And there upon the ground I sit,
    And sing a song to them.     44

"And often after sunset, Sir,
    When it is light and fair,
I take my little porringer,
    And eat my supper there.     48

"The first that died was sister Jane;
    In bed she moaning lay,
Till God released her of her pain;
    And then she went away.     52

"So in the church-yard she was laid;
    And, when the grass was dry,
Together round her grave we played,
    My brother John and I.     56

"And when the ground was white with
    snow,
    And I could run and slide,
My brother John was forced to go,
    And he lies by her side."     60

"How many are you, then," said I,
    "If they two are in heaven?"

Quick was the little Maid's reply,
  "O Master! we are seven."                    64

"But they are dead; those two are dead!
  Their spirits are in heaven!"
'T was throwing words away; for still
The little Maid would have her will,
  And said, "Nay, we are seven!"               68

1798.                            *William Wordsworth.*


# LUCY GRAY

### OR, SOLITUDE

OFT I had heard of Lucy Gray:
  And, when I crossed the wild,
I chanced to see at break of day
  The solitary child.                          4

No mate, no comrade Lucy knew;
  She dwelt on a wide moor,
—The sweetest thing that ever grew
  Beside a human door!                         8

You yet may spy the fawn at play,
  The hare upon the green;
But the sweet face of Lucy Gray
  Will never more be seen.                     12

"To-night will be a stormy night—
   You to the town must go;
And take a lantern, Child, to light
   Your mother through the snow."    16

"That, Father! will I gladly do:
   'T is scarcely afternoon—
The minster-clock has just struck two,
   And yonder is the moon!"    20

At this the Father raised his hook,
   And snapped a fagot-band;
He plied his work;—and Lucy took
   The lantern in her hand.    24

Not blither is the mountain roe:
   With many a wanton stroke
Her feet disperse the powdery snow,
   That rises up like smoke.    28

The storm came on before its time:
   She wandered up and down;
And many a hill did Lucy climb:
   But never reached the town.    32

The wretched parents all that night
   Went shouting far and wide;
But there was neither sound nor sight
   To serve them for a guide.    36

At day-break on the hill they stood
   That overlooked the moor;

And thence they saw the bridge of wood,
  A furlong from their door.      40


They wept—and, turning homeward,
    cried,
"In heaven we all shall meet;"
—When in the snow the mother spied
  The print of Lucy's feet.      44


Then downwards from the steep hill's
    edge
  They tracked the footmarks small;
And through the broken hawthorn hedge,
  And by the long stone-wall;      48


And then an open field they crossed:
  The marks were still the same;
They tracked them on, nor ever lost;
  And to the bridge they came.      52


They followed from the snowy bank
  Those footmarks, one by one,
Into the middle of the plank;
  And further there were none!      56


—Yet some maintain that to this day
  She is a living child;
That you may see sweet Lucy Gray
  Upon the lonesome wild.      60

O'er rough and smooth she trips along,
    And never looks behind;
And sings a solitary song
    That whistles in the wind.           64
1800.                           *William Wordsworth.*


# PROUD MAISIE

### From *The Heart of* **Mid-Lothian**

PROUD Maisie is in the wood,
    Walking so early;
Sweet Robin sits on the bush,
    Singing so rarely.           4


"Tell me, thou bonny bird,
    When shall I marry me?"—
"When six braw gentlemen
    Kirkward shall carry ye."           8


"Who makes the bridal bed,
    Birdie, say truly?"—
"The gray-headed sexton
    That delves the grave duly.           12


"The glow-worm o'er grave and stone
    Shall light thee steady.
The owl from the steeple sing,
    'Welcome, proud lady.'"           16
1818.                           *Sir Walter Scott.*

# LORD ULLIN'S DAUGHTER

A CHIEFTAIN to the Highlands bound
   Cries, "Boatman, do not tarry!
And I'll give thee a silver pound
   To row us o'er the ferry!"—

"Now who be ye, would cross Lochgyle,
   This dark and stormy water?"
"O, I'm the chief of Ulva's isle,
   And this, Lord Ullin's daughter.—    8

"And fast before her father's men
   Three days we've fled together,
For should he find us in the glen,
   My blood would stain the heather.    12

"His horsemen hard behind us ride;
   Should they our steps discover,
Then who will cheer my bonny bride
   When they have slain her lover?"—    16

Out spoke the hardy Highland wight—
   "I'll go, my chief—I'm ready:—
It is not for your silver bright;
   But for your winsome lady:    20

259

"And by my word! the bonny bird
    In danger shall not tarry;
So though the waves are raging white,
    I 'll row you o'er the ferry."—                24


By this the storm grew loud apace,
    The water-wraith was shrieking;
And in the scowl of heaven each face
    Grew dark as they were speaking.            28


But still as wilder blew the wind,
    And as the night grew drearer,
Adown the glen rode armèd men,
    Their trampling sounded nearer.—           32


"O haste thee, haste!" the lady cries,
    "Though tempests round us gather;
I 'll meet the raging of the skies,
    But not an angry father."—                    36


The boat has left a stormy land,
    A stormy sea before her,—
When, O! too strong for human hand,
    The tempest gather'd o'er her.                40


And still they row'd amidst the roar
    Of waters fast prevailing:
Lord Ullin reach'd that fatal shore,—
    His wrath was changed to wailing.           44

# The Sands of Dee

For, sore dismay'd, through storm and
    shade,
  His child he did discover:—
One lovely hand she stretch'd for aid,
  And one was round her lover.    48

"Come back! come back!" he cried in grief
  "Across this stormy water:
And I'll forgive your Highland chief,
  My daughter!—O my daughter!"    52

'T was vain: the loud waves lash'd the
    shore,
  Return or aid preventing:
The waters wild went o'er his child,
  And he was left lamenting.    56

*1804.*                       *Thomas Campbell.*


# THE SANDS OF DEE

"O MARY, go and call the cattle home,
  And call the cattle home,
  And call the cattle home,
  Across the sands of Dee!"
The western wind was wild and dank with
    foam,
  And all alone went she.    6

The western tide crept up along the sand,
  And o'er and o'er the sand,
  And round and round the sand,

As far as eye could see.
The rolling mist came down and hid the land:
And never home came she.          12

"Oh! is it weed, or fish, or floating hair—
A tress of golden hair,
A drownèd maiden's hair
Above the nets at sea?
Was never salmon yet that shone so fair
Among the stakes on Dee."          18

They rowed her in across the rolling foam,
The cruel, crawling foam,
The cruel, hungry foam,
To her grave beside the sea:
But still the boatmen hear her call the cattle
home
Across the sands of Dee.          24

1849.                         *Charles Kingsley.*


# THE THREE FISHERS

THREE fishers went sailing away to the West,
Away to the West as the sun went down;
Each thought on the woman who loved him the
best,
And the children stood watching them out of
the town;
For men must work, and women must weep,
And there's little to earn, and many to keep,
Though the harbour bar be moaning.          7

## High-tide on Coast of Lincolnshire

Three wives sat up in the light-house tower,
  And trimmed the lamps as the sun went down;
They looked at the squall, and they looked at the
      shower,
  And the night-rack came rolling up ragged and
      brown.
But men must work, and women must weep,
Though storms be sudden, and waters deep,
    And the harbour bar be moaning.          14

Three corpses lay out on the shining sands
  In the morning gleam as the tide went down,
And the women are weeping and wringing their
      hands
  For those who will never come home to the
      town;
For men must work, and women must weep,
And the sooner it's over, the sooner to sleep;
    And good-bye to the bar and its moaning.   21

*1851.*                      *Charles Kingsley.*


# THE HIGH-TIDE ON THE COAST OF LINCOLNSHIRE. [TIME, 1571.]

THE old mayor climbed the belfry tower,
  The ringers ran by two, by three;
"Pull! if ye never pulled before;
  Good ringers, pull your best," quoth he.
"Play uppe, play uppe, O Boston bells!
Ply all your changes, all your swells!
  Play uppe *The Brides of Enderby!*"      7

Men say it was a " stolen tyde,"—
　　The Lord that sent it, he knows all,
But in myne ears doth still abide
　　The message that the bells let fall;
And there was naught of strange, beside
The flights of mews and peewits pied,
　　By millions crouched on the old sea-wall.　　14

I sat and spun within the doore;
　　My thread brake off, I raised myne eyes:
The level sun, like ruddy ore,
　　Lay sinking in the barren skies;
And dark against day's golden death
She moved where Lindis wandereth,—
My sonne's faire wife, Elizabeth.　　21

" Cusha! Cusha! Cusha!" calling,
　　Ere the early dews were falling,
Farre away I heard her song.
" Cusha! Cusha!" all along;
　　Where the reedy Lindis floweth,
　　　　Floweth, floweth,
From the meads where melick groweth,
Faintly came her milking-song.　　29

" Cusha! Cusha! Cusha!" calling,
" For the dews will soone be falling;
Leave your meadow grasses mellow,
　　　　Mellow, mellow!
Quit your cowslips, cowslips yellow!
Come uppe, Whitefoot! come uppe, Lightfoot!
Quit the stalks of parsley hollow,
　　　　Hollow, hollow!

# High-tide on Coast of Lincolnshire

Come uppe, Jetty! rise and follow;
From the clovers lift your head!
Come uppe, Whitefoot! come uppe, Lightfoot!
Come uppe, Jetty! rise and follow,
Jetty, to the milking-shed."      42

If it be long—aye, long ago—
  When I beginne to think howe long,
Againe I hear the Lindis flow,
  Swift as an arrowe, sharpe and strong;
And all the aire, it seemeth mee,
Bin full of floating bells (sayth shee),
That ring the tune of *Enderby*.      49

Alle fresh the level pasture lay,
  And not a shadowe mote be seene,
Save where, full fyve good miles away,
  The steeple towered from out the greene.
And lo! the great bell farre and wide
Was heard in all the country side
That Saturday at eventide.      56

The swannerds, where their sedges are,
  Moved on in sunset's golden breath;
The shepherde lads I heard afarre,
  And my sonne's wife, Elizabeth;
Till, floating o'er the grassy sea,
Came downe that kyndly message free,
*The Brides of Mavis Enderby*.      63

Then some looked uppe into the sky,
  And all along where Lindis flows

To where the goodly vessels lie,
    And where the lordly steeple shows.
They sayde, " And why should this thing be,
What danger lowers by land or sea?
They ring the tune of *Enderby*.                70

" For evil news from Mablethorpe,
    Of pyrate galleys, warping down, —
For shippes ashore beyond the scorpe,
    They have not spared to wake the towne;
But while the west bin red to see,
And storms be none, and pyrates flee,
Why ring *The Brides of Enderby?* "            77

I looked without, and lo! my sonne
    Came riding downe with might and main;
He raised a shout as he drew on,
    Till all the welkin rang again:
" Elizabeth! Elizabeth!"
(A sweeter woman ne'er drew breath
Than my sonne's wife, Elizabeth.)             84

" The olde sea-wall (he cryed) is downe!
    The rising tide comes on apace;
And boats adrift in yonder towne
    Go sailing uppe the market-place!"
He shook as one that looks on death:
" God save you, mother!" straight he sayth;
" Where is my wife, Elizabeth?"               91

" Good sonne, where Lindis winds away
    With her two bairns I marked her long;

266

And ere yon bells beganne to play,
  Afar I heard her milking-song."
He looked across the grassy sea,
To right, to left, *Ho, Enderby!*
They rang *The Brides of Enderby.*    98

With that he cried and beat his breast;
  For lo! along the river's bed
A mighty eygre reared his crest,
  And uppe the Lindis raging sped.
It swept with thunderous noises loud, —
Shaped like a curling snow-white cloud,
Or like a demon in a shroud.    105

And rearing Lindis, backward pressed,
  Shook all her trembling bankes amaine;
Then madly at the eygre's breast
  Flung uppe her weltering walls again.
Then bankes came downe with ruin and rout, —
Then beaten foam flew round about, —
Then all the mighty floods were out.    112

So farre, so fast, the eygre drave,
  The heart had hardly time to beat,
Before a shallow seething wave
  Sobbed in the grasses at oure feet:
The feet had hardly time to flee
Before it brake against the knee, —
And all the world was in the sea.    119

Upon the roofe we sate that night;
  The noise of bells went sweeping by;

I marked the lofty beacon light
　　Stream from the church-tower, red and high,—
A lurid mark, and dread to see;
　　And awsome bells they were to mee,
That in the dark rang *Enderby*.　　　　126


They rang the sailor lads to guide,
　　From roofe to roofe who fearless rowed;
And I, — my sonne was at my side,
　　And yet the ruddy beacon glowed;
And yet he moaned beneath his breath,
"O come in life, or come in death!
O lost! my love, Elizabeth!"　　　　133


And didst thou visit him no more?
　　Thou didst, thou didst, my daughter deare;
The waters laid thee at his doore,
　　Ere the early dawn was clear.
Thy pretty bairns in fast embrace,
The lifted sun shone on thy face,
Downe drifted to thy dwelling-place.　　　　140


That flow strewed wrecks about the grass,
　　That ebbe swept out the flocks to sea, —
A fatal ebbe and flow, alas!
　　To manye more than myne and mee;
But each will mourne his own (she saith)
And sweeter woman ne'er drew breath
Than my sonne's wife, Elizabeth.　　　　147


I shall never hear her more
By the reedy Lindis shore,

# High-tide on Coast of Lincolnshire

"Cusha! Cusha! Cusha!" calling,
  Ere the early dews be falling;
  I shall never hear her song,
"Cusha! Cusha!" all along,
  Where the sunny Lindis floweth,
       Goeth, floweth,
  From the meads where melick groweth,
  Where the water, winding down,
  Onward floweth to the town.     158

I shall never see her more,
  Where the reeds and rushes quiver,
       Shiver, quiver,
  Stand beside the sobbing river,—
  Sobbing, throbbing, in its falling,
  To the sandy, lonesome shore;
  I shall never hear her calling,
"Leave your meadow grasses mellow,
       Mellow, mellow!
  Quit your cowslips, cowslips yellow!
  Come uppe, Whitefoot! come uppe, Lightfoot!
  Quit your pipes of parsley hollow,
       Hollow, hollow!
  Come uppe, Lightfoot! rise and follow;
       Lightfoot! Whitefoot!
  From your clovers lift the head;
  Come uppe, Jetty! follow, follow,
  Jetty, to the milking-shed!"     176

1863.            *Jean Ingelow.*

# THE EXECUTION OF MONTROSE

COME hither, Evan Cameron!
  Come, stand behind my knee —
I hear the river roaring down
  Towards the wintry sea.
There 's shouting on the mountain-side,
  There 's war within the blast —
Old faces look upon me,
  Old forms go trooping past:
I hear the pibroch wailing
  Amidst the din of fight,
And my dim spirit wakes again
  Upon the verge of night.      12

'T was I that led the Highland host
  Through wild Lochaber's snows,
What time the plaided clans came down
  To battle with Montrose.
I 've told thee how the Southrons fell
  Beneath the broad claymore,
And how we smote the Campbell clan
  By Inverlochy's shore.
I 've told thee how we swept Dundee,
  And tamed the Lindsays' pride;
But never have I told thee yet
  How the great Marquis died.      24

# The Execution of Montrose

A traitor sold him to his foes;
  O deed of deathless shame!
I charge thee, boy, if e'er thou meet
  With one of Assynt's name —
Be it upon the mountain's side,
  Or yet within the glen,
Stand he in martial gear alone,
  Or backed by armèd men —
Face him, as thou wouldst face the man
  Who wronged thy sire's renown;
Remember of what blood thou art,
  And strike the caitiff down!      36


They brought him to the Watergate,
  Hard bound with hempen span,
As though they held a lion there,
  And not a fenceless man.
They set him high upon a cart —
  The hangman rode below —
They drew his hands behind his back,
  And bared his noble brow.
Then, as a hound is slipped from leash,
  They cheered the common throng,
And blew the note with yell and shout,
  And bade him pass along.      48


It would have made a brave man's heart
  Grow sad and sick that day,
To watch the keen malignant eyes
  Bent down on that array.
There stood the Whig west-country lords,
  In balcony and bow;

There sat their gaunt and withered dames,
　And their daughters all a-row.
And every open window
　Was full as full might be
With black-robed Covenanting carles,
　That goodly sport to see!　　　　　　60


But when he came, though pale and wan,
　He looked so great and high,
So noble was his manly front,
　So calm his steadfast eye; —
The rabble rout forbore to shout,
　And each man held his breath,
For well they knew the hero's soul
　Was face to face with death.
And then a mournful shudder
　Through all the people crept,
And some that came to scoff at him
　Now turned aside and wept.　　　　　72


But onward — always onward,
　In silence and in gloom,
The dreary pageant laboured,
　Till it reached the house of doom.
Then first a woman's voice was heard
　In jeer and laughter loud,
And an angry cry and a hiss arose
　From the heart of the tossing crowd:
Then as the Græme looked upward,
　He saw the ugly smile
Of him who sold his king for gold —
　The master-fiend Argyle!　　　　　84

# The Execution of Montrose

The Marquis gazed a moment,
  And nothing did he say,
But the cheek of Argyle grew ghastly pale,
  And he turned his eyes away.
The painted harlot by his side,
  She shook through every limb,
For a roar like thunder swept the street,
  And hands were clenched at him;
And a Saxon soldier cried aloud,
  "Back, coward, from thy place!
For seven long years thou hast not dared
  To look him in the face."          96


Had I been there with sword in hand,
  And fifty Camerons by,
That day through high Dunedin's streets
  Had pealed the slogan-cry.
Not all their troops of trampling horse,
  Nor might of mailèd men —
Not all the rebels in the south
  Had borne us backwards then!
Once more his foot on Highland heath
  Had trod as free as air,
Or I, and all who bore my name,
  Been laid around him there!          108


It might not be. They placed him next
  Within the solemn hall,
Where once the Scottish kings were throned
  Amidst their nobles all.
But there was dust of vulgar feet
  On that polluted floor,

273

And perjured traitors filled the place
  Where good men sate before.
With savage glee came Warristoun
  To read the murderous doom;
And then uprose the great Montrose
  In the middle of the room.        120

"Now, by my faith as belted knight,
  And by the name I bear,
And by the bright Saint Andrew's cross
  That waves above us there —
Yea, by a greater, mightier oath —
  And Oh, that such should be!—
By that dark stream of royal blood
  That lies 'twixt you and me —
I have not sought in battle-field
  A wreath of such renown,
Nor dared I hope on my dying day
  To win the martyr's crown!       132

"There is a chamber far away
  Where sleep the good and brave,
But a better place ye have named for me
  Than by my father's grave.
For truth and right, 'gainst treason's might,
  This hand hath always striven,
And ye raise it up for a witness still
  In the eye of earth and heaven.
Then nail my head on yonder tower —
  Give every town a limb —
And God who made shall gather them:
  I go from you to Him!"       144

BENAWE, LOCH ETIVE, IN ARGYLESHIRE

# The Execution of Montrose

The morning dawned full darkly,
  The rain came flashing down,
And the jagged streak of the levin-bolt
  Lit up the gloomy town:
The thunder crashed across the heaven,
  The fatal hour was come;
Yet aye broke in with muffled beat,
  The 'larum of the drum.
There was madness on the earth below
  And anger in the sky,
And young and old, and rich and poor,
  Came forth to see him die.                    156


Ah, God! that ghastly gibbet!
  How dismal 't is to see
The great tall spectral skeleton,
  The ladder and the tree!
Hark! hark! it is the clash of arms—
  The bells begin to toll—
"He is coming! he is coming!
  God's mercy on his soul!"
One last long peal of thunder—
  The clouds are cleared away,
And the glorious sun once more looks down
  Amidst the dazzling day.                      168


"He is coming! he is coming!"
  Like a bridegroom from his room,
Came the hero from his prison
  To the scaffold and the doom.
There was glory on his forehead,
  There was lustre in his eye,

And he never walked to battle
    More proudly than to die:
There was colour in his visage,
    Though the cheeks of all were **wan**;
And they marvelled as they saw him pass,
    That great and goodly man!                      180

He mounted up the scaffold,
    And he turned him to the crowd;
But they dared not trust the people,
    So he might not speak aloud.
But he looked upon the heavens,
    And they were clear and blue,
And in the liquid ether
    The eye of God shone through!
Yet a black and murky battlement
    Lay resting on the hill,
As though the thunder slept within—
    All else was calm and still.                    192

The grim Geneva ministers
    With anxious scowl drew near,
As you have seen the ravens flock
    Around the dying deer.
He would not deign them word nor sign,
    But alone he bent the knee;
And veiled his face for Christ's dear grace
    Beneath the gallows-tree.
Then radiant and serene he rose,
    And cast his cloak away:
For he had ta'en his latest look
    Of earth and sun and day.                       204

276

## The Shameful Death

A beam of light fell o'er him,
  Like a glory round the shriven,
And he climbed the lofty ladder
  As it were the path to heaven.
Then came a flash from out the cloud,
  And a stunning thunder-roll;
And no man dared to look aloft,
  For fear was on every soul.
There was another heavy sound,
  A hush and then a groan;
And darkness swept across the sky—
  The work of death was done!                    216

1848.                        *William Edmondstoune Aytoun.*


## THE SHAMEFUL DEATH

There were four of us about that bed;
  The mass-priest knelt at the side,
I and his mother stood at the head,
  Over his feet lay the bride;
We were quite sure that he was dead,
  Though his eyes were open wide.                    6

He did not die in the night,
  He did not die in the day,
But in the morning twilight
  His spirit pass'd away,
When neither sun nor moon was bright,
  And the trees were merely gray.                    12

He was not slain with the sword,
   Knight's axe, or the knightly spear,
Yet spoke he never a word
   After he came in here;
I cut away the cord
   From the neck of my brother dear.    18

He did not strike one blow,
   For the recreants came behind,
In the place where the hornbeams grow,
   A path right hard to find,
For the hornbeam boughs swing so,
   That the twilight makes it blind.    24

They lighted a great torch then,
   When his arms were pinion'd fast,
Sir John the knight of the Fen,
   Sir Guy of the Dolorous Blast,
With knights threescore and ten,
   Hung brave Lord Hugh at last.    30

I am threescore and ten,
   And my hair is all turn'd grey,
But I met Sir John of the Fen
   Long ago on a summer day,
And am glad to think of the moment when
   I took his life away.    36

I am threescore and ten,
   And my strength is mostly pass'd,
But long ago I and my men,
   When the sky was overcast,

# Rizpah

And the smoke roll'd over the reeds of the
    fen,
    Slew Guy of the Dolorous Blast.     **42**

And now, knights all of you,
    I pray you pray for Sir Hugh,
A good knight and a true,
    And for Alice, his wife, pray too.   **46**

1858.                  *William Morris.*


## RIZPAH

### 17—

WAILING, wailing, wailing, the wind over land
    and sea—
And Willy's voice in the wind, "O mother,
    come out to me!"
Why should he call me to-night, when he
    knows that I cannot go?
For the downs are as bright as day, and the full
    moon stares at the snow.     **4**

We should be seen, my dear; they would spy us
    out of the town.
The loud black nights for us, and the storm
    rushing over the down,
When I cannot see my own hand, but am led
    by the creak of the chain,
And grovel and grope for my son till I find my-
    self drenched with the rain.    **8**

Anything fallen again? nay—what was there
    left to fall?
I have taken them home, I have number'd the
    bones, I have hidden them all.
What am I saying? and what are *you?* do you
    come as a spy?
Falls? what falls? who knows? As the tree
    falls so must it lie.    12


Who let her in? how long has she been? you—
    what have you heard?
Why did you sit so quiet? you never have
    spoken a word.
O—to pray with me—yes—a lady—none of
    their spies—
But the night has crept into my heart, and
    begun to darken my eyes.    16


Ah—you, that have lived so soft, what should
    *you* know of the night,
The blast and the burning shame and the bitter
    frost and the fright?
I have done it, while you were asleep—you
    were only made for the day.
I have gather'd my baby together—and now
    you may go your way.    20


Nay—for it's kind of you, Madam, to sit by an
    old dying wife.
But say nothing hard of my boy, I have only an
    hour of life.

# Rizpah

I kiss'd my boy in the prison, before he went
    out to die.
"They dared me to do it," he said, and he never
    has told me a lie.
I whipt him for robbing an orchard once when
    he was but a child—
"The farmer dared me to do it," he said; he was
    always so wild—
And idle—and could n't be idle—my Willy—
    he never could rest.
The King should have made him a soldier, he
    would have been one of his best.     28

But he lived with a lot of wild mates, and they
    never would let him be good;
They swore that he dare not rob the mail, and
    he swore that he would;
And he took no life, but he took one purse, and
    when all was done
He flung it among his fellows—"I 'll none of
    it," said my son.     32

I came into court to the Judge and the lawyers.
    I told them my tale,
God's own truth—but they kill'd him, they
    kill'd him for robbing the mail.
They hang'd him in chains for a show—we had
    always borne a good name—
To be hang'd for a thief—and then put away—
    is n't that enough shame?
Dust to dust—low down—let us hide! but
    they set him so high

That all the ships of the world could stare at
    him, passing by.
God 'll pardon the hell-black raven and horrible
    fowls of the air,
But not the black heart of the lawyer who
    kill'd him and hang'd him there.    40

And the jailer forced me away.  I had bid him
    my last good bye;
They had fasten'd the door of his cell.  " O
    mother ! " I heard him cry.
I could n't get back tho' I tried, he had some-
    thing further to say,
And now I never shall know it.  The jailer
    forced me away.    44

Then since I could n't but hear that cry of my
    boy that was dead,
They seized me and shut me up: they fasten'd
    me down on my bed.
" Mother, O mother ! "—he call'd in the dark to
    me year after year—
They beat me for that, they beat me—you know
    that I could n't but hear;
And then at the last they found I had grown so
    stupid and still
They let me abroad again—but the creatures
    had worked their will.    50

Flesh of my flesh was gone, but bone of my
    bone was left—
I stole them all from the lawyers—and you,
    will you call it a theft?—

# Rizpah

My baby, the bones that had suck'd me, the
    bones that had laugh'd and had cried—
Theirs?  O, no! they are mine—not theirs—
    they had moved in my side.    54


Do you think I was scared by the bones?  I
    kiss'd 'em, I buried 'em all—
I can't dig deep, I am old—in the night by the
    churchyard wall.
My Willy 'll rise up whole when the trumpet
    of judgment 'll sound;
But I charge you never to say that I laid him
    in holy ground.    58


They would scratch him up—they would hang
    him again on the cursed tree.
Sin?  O yes, we are sinners, I know—let all
    that be,
And read me a Bible verse of the Lord's good-
    will toward men—
" Full of compassion and mercy, the Lord "—let
    me hear it again;
" Full of compassion and mercy—long-suffering."
    Yes, O yes!
For the lawyer is born but to murder—the
    Saviour lives but to bless.
*He* 'll never put on the black cap except for the
    worst of the worst,
And the first may be last—I have heard it in
    church—and the last may be first.

Suffering—O, long-suffering—yes, as the Lord
    must know,
Year after year in the mist and the wind and
    the shower and the snow.     68


Heard, have you? what? they have told you he
    never repented his sin.
How do they know it? are *they* his mother?
    are *you* of his kin?
Heard! have you ever heard, when the storm
    on the downs began,
The wind that'ill wail like a child and the sea
    that'ill moan like a man?     72


Election, Election, and Reprobation—it's all
    very well.
But I go to-night to my boy, and I shall not find
    him in Hell.
For I cared so much for my boy that the Lord
    has look'd into my care,
And He means me I'm sure to be happy with
    Willy, I know not where.     76


And if *he* be lost—but to save *my* soul, that is
    all your desire—
Do you think that I care for *my* soul if my boy
    be gone to the fire?
I have been with God in the dark—go, go, you
    may leave me alone—
You never have borne a child—you are just as
    hard as a stone.     80

# The Raven

Madam, I beg your pardon! I think that you
    mean to be kind,
But I cannot hear what you say for my Willy's
    voice is in the wind—
The snow and the sky so bright—he used but
    to call in the dark,
And he calls to me now from the church and
    not from the gibbet—for hark!
Nay—you can hear it yourself—it is coming—
    shaking the walls—
Willy—the moon's in a cloud——Good night.
    I am going. He calls.        86

1880.                     *Lord Tennyson.*


# THE RAVEN

Once upon a midnight dreary, while I pondered,
    weak and weary,
Over many a quaint and curious volume of for-
    gotten lore,—
While I nodded, nearly napping, suddenly there
    came a tapping,
As of some one gently rapping, rapping at my
    chamber door.
"'T is some visitor," I muttered, "tapping at my
    chamber door;
      Only this, and nothing more."     6

Ah, distinctly I remember, it was in the bleak
    December,
And each separate dying ember wrought its
    ghost upon the floor.
Eagerly I wished the morrow; vainly I had
    sought to borrow
From my books surcease of sorrow,—sorrow
    for the lost Lenore,—
For the rare and radiant maiden whom the
    angels named Lenore,—
        Nameless here for evermore.    12

And the silken, sad, uncertain rustling of each
    purple curtain
Thrilled me,—filled me with fantastic terrors
    never felt before;
So that now, to still the beating of my heart, I
    stood repeating,
" 'T is some visitor entreating entrance at my
    chamber door,—
Some late visitor entreating entrance at my
    chamber door;
        That it is, and nothing more."    18

Presently my soul grew stronger; hesitating
    then no longer,
" Sir," said I, " or Madam, truly your forgive-
    ness I implore;
But the fact is, I was napping, and so gently
    you came rapping,
And so faintly you came tapping, tapping at my
    chamber door,

# The Raven

That I scarce was sure I heard you "—Here I
    opened wide the door;
      Darkness there, and nothing more.    24

Deep into that darkness peering, long I stood
    there, wondering, fearing,
Doubting, dreaming dreams no mortal ever
    dared to dream before;
But the silence was unbroken, and the darkness
    gave no token,
And the only word there spoken was the whis-
    pered word "Lenore!"
This I whispered, and an echo murmured back
    the word "Lenore!"
      Merely this, and nothing more.    30

Back into the chamber turning, all my soul
    within me burning,
Soon again I heard a tapping, something louder
    than before.
"Surely," said I, "surely that is something at my
    window-lattice;
Let me see then what thereat is, and this mys-
    tery explore,—
Let my heart be still a moment, and this mys-
    tery explore;—
      'T is the wind, and nothing more."    36

Open here I flung the shutter, when, with many
    a flirt and flutter,
In there stepped a stately Raven of the saintly
    days of yore.

Not the least obeisance made he; not an instant
    stopped or stayed he;
But, with mien of lord or lady, perched above
    my chamber door,—
Perched upon a bust of Pallas, just above my
    chamber door,—
        Perched, and sat, and nothing more.   42

Then this ebony bird beguiling my sad fancy
    into smiling,
By the grave and stern decorum of the counte-
    nance it wore,
" Though thy crest be shorn and shaven, thou,"
    I said, " art sure no craven ;
Ghastly, grim, and ancient Raven, wandering
    from the Nightly shore,
Tell me what thy lordly name is on the Night's
    Plutonian shore ? "
        Quoth the Raven, " Nevermore ! "   48

Much I marvelled this ungainly fowl to hear
    discourse so plainly,
Though its answer little meaning, little rele-
    vancy bore ;
For we cannot help agreeing that no living
    human being
Ever yet was blessed with seeing bird above his
    chamber door,
Bird or beast upon the sculptured bust above
    his chamber door,
        With such name as " Nevermore ! "   54

# The Raven

But the Raven, sitting lonely on the placid bust,
    spoke only
That one word, as if his soul in that one word
    he did outpour.
Nothing further then he uttered,—not a feather
    then he fluttered,—
Till I scarcely more than muttered, "Other
    friends have flown before,—
On the morrow *he* will leave me, as my Hopes
    have flown before."
        Then the bird said, "Nevermore!"   60

Startled at the stillness broken by reply so
    aptly spoken,
"Doubtless," said I, "what it utters is its only
    stock and store,
Caught from some unhappy master whom un-
    merciful Disaster
Followed fast and followed faster, till his song
    one burden bore,
Till the dirges of his Hope that melancholy bur-
    den bore,—
        Of 'Never—nevermore!'"   66

But the Raven still beguiling all my sad soul
    into smiling,
Straight I wheeled a cushioned seat in front of
    bird and bust and door,
Then, upon the velvet sinking, I betook myself
    to linking
Fancy unto fancy, thinking what this ominous
    bird of yore—

What this grim, ungainly, ghastly, gaunt, and
    ominous bird of yore —
        Meant in croaking "Nevermore!"    72

This I sat engaged in guessing, but no syllable
    expressing
To the fowl whose fiery eyes now burned into
    my bosom's core;
This and more I sat divining, with my head at
    ease reclining
On the cushion's velvet lining that the lamp-
    light gloated o'er,
But whose velvet violet lining, with the lamp-
    light gloating o'er,
        *She* shall press—ah! nevermore!    78

Then methought the air grew denser, perfumed
    from an unseen censer,
Swung by Seraphim, whose footfalls tinkled on
    the tufted floor.
"Wretch," I cried, "thy God hath lent thee,—by
    these angels he hath sent thee
Respite,—respite and nepenthe from thy memo-
    ries of Lenore!
Quaff, oh, quaff this kind nepenthe, and forget
    this lost Lenore!"
        Quoth the Raven, "Nevermore!"    84

"Prophet!" said I, "thing of evil!—prophet
    still, if bird or devil!
Whether Tempter sent, or whether tempest
    tossed thee here ashore,

# The Raven

Desolate yet all undaunted, on this desert land
   enchanted,—
On this home by Horror haunted,—tell me
   truly, I implore,—
Is there—*is* there balm in Gilead?—tell me,—
   tell me, I implore!"
    Quoth the Raven, "Nevermore!"   90

"Prophet!" said I, "thing of evil!—prophet
   still, if bird or devil!
By that heaven that bends above us,—by that
   God we both adore,
Tell this soul with sorrow laden, if, within the
   distant Aidenn,
It shall clasp a sainted maiden, whom the an-
   gels name Lenore,
Clasp a rare and radiant maiden, whom the
   angels name Lenore!"
    Quoth the Raven, "Nevermore!"   96

"Be that word our sign of parting, bird or
   fiend!" I shrieked, upstarting,—
"Get thee back into the tempest and the Night's
   Plutonian shore!
Leave no black plume as a token of that lie thy
   soul hath spoken!
Leave my loneliness unbroken!—quit the bust
   above my door!
Take thy beak from out my heart, and take thy
   form from off my door!"
    Quoth the Raven, "Nevermore!"   102

And the Raven, never flitting, still is sitting,
   still is sitting
On the pallid bust of Pallas, just above my
   chamber door;
And his eyes have all the seeming of a demon's
   that is dreaming,
And the lamplight o'er him streaming throws
   his shadow on the floor;
And my soul from out that shadow that lies
   floating on the floor
      Shall be lifted—*nevermore!*                    108

1845.                                    *Edgar Allan Poe.*

# SELECTIONS
# FROM THE LATER POETRY

*Ballads*
*Love*
*The Sea*
*War*
*Death and Sorrow*

# THE BALLAD OF CAMDEN TOWN

I WALKED with Maisie long years back
　The streets of Camden Town,
I splendid in my suit of black,
　And she divine in brown.　　　　4

Hers was a proud and noble face,
　A secret heart and eyes
Like water in a lonely place
　Beneath unclouded skies.　　　　8

A bed, a chest, a faded mat,
　And broken chairs a few.
Were all we had to grace our flat
　In Hazel Avenue.　　　　12

But I could walk to Hampstead Heath,
　And crown her head with daisies,
And watch the streaming world beneath,
　And men with other Maisies.　　　　16

When I was ill and she was pale
　And empty stood our store,
She left the latch key on its nail,
　And saw me nevermore.　　　　20

Perhaps she cast herself away
    Lest both of us should drown:
Perhaps she feared to die, as they
    Who die in Camden Town.    24

What 'came of her?   The bitter nights
    Destroy the rose and lily,
And souls are lost among the lights
    Of painted Piccadilly.    28

What 'came of her?   The river flows
    So deep and wide and stilly,
And waits to catch the fallen rose
    And clasp the broken lily.    32

I dream she dwells in London still
    And breathes the evening air,
And often walk to Primrose Hill,
    And hope to meet her there.    36

Once more together we will live,
    For I will find her yet;
I have so little to forgive;
    So much I can't forget.    40

*James Elroy Flecker.*


# THE PROUD LADY

WHEN Stävoren town was in its prime
    And queened the Zuyder Zee,
Its ships went out to every clime
    With costly merchantry.    4

# The Proud Lady

A lady dwelt in that rich town,
   The fairest in all the land;
She walked abroad in a velvet gown,
   With many rings on her hand.     8

Her hair was bright as the beaten gold,
   Her lips as coral red,
Her roving eyes were blue and bold,
   And her heart with pride was fed.     12

For she was proud of her father's ships,
   As she watched them gayly pass;
And pride looked out of her eyes and lips
   When she saw herself in the glass.     16

"Now come," she said to the captains ten,
   Who were ready to put to sea,
"Ye are all my men and my father's men,
   And what will ye do for me?"     20

"Go north and south, go east and west,
   And get me gifts," she said.
"And he who bringeth me home the best,
   With that man will I wed."     24

So they all fared forth, and sought with care
   In many a famous mart,
For satins and silks and jewels rare,
   To win that lady's heart.     28

She looked at them all with never a thought,
   And careless put them by;

"I am not fain of the things ye brought,
   Enough of these have I."     32

The last that came was the head of the fleet,
   His name was Jan Borel;
He bent his knee at the lady's feet,—
   In truth he loved her well.    36

"I've brought thee home the best i' the world,
   A shipful of Danzig corn!"
She stared at him long; her red lips curled,
   Her blue eyes filled with scorn.    40

"Now out on thee, thou feckless kerl,
   A loon thou art," she said.
"Am I a starving beggar girl?
   Shall I ever lack for bread?    44

"Go empty all thy sacks of grain
   Into the nearest sea,
And never show thy face again
   To make a mock of me."    48

Young Jan Borel, he answered naught,
   But in the harbor cast
The sacks of golden corn he brought,
   And groaned when fell the last.    52

Then Jan Borel, he hoisted sail,
   And out to sea he bore;
He passed the Helder in a gale
   And came again no more.    56

# The Proud Lady

But the grains of corn went drifting down
  Like devil-scattered seed,
To sow the harbor of the town
  With a wicked growth of weed.          60

The roots were thick and the silt and sand
  Were gathered day by day,
ill not a furlong out from land
  A shoal had barred the way.            64

The Stävoren town saw evil years,
  No ships could out or in,
The boats lay rotting at the piers,
  And the mouldy grain in the bin.       68

The grass-grown streets were all forlorn,
  The town in ruin stood,
The lady's velvet gown was torn,
  Her rings were sold for food.          72

Her father had perished long ago,
  But the lady held her pride,
She walked with a scornful step and slow,
  Till at last in her rags she died.     76

Yet still on the crumbling piers of the town,
  When the midnight moon shines free,
A woman walks in a velvet gown
  And scatters corn in the sea.          80

*Henry van Dyke.*

# THE EARL O' QUARTERDECK*

### *A New Old Ballad*

THE wind it blew, and the ship it flew;
   And it was "Hey for hame!
And ho for hame!"  But the skipper cried,
   "Haud her oot o'er the saut sea faem."    4


Then up and spoke the King himsel':
   "Haud on for Dunfermline!"
Quo the skipper, "Ye're king upon' the land—
   I'm king upo' the brine."    8


And he took the helm intil his hand,
   And he steered the ship sae free;
Wi' the wind astarn, he crowded sail,
   And stood right out to sea.    12


Quo the king, "There's treason in this I vow;
   This is something underhand!
'Bout ship!"  Quo the skipper, "Yer grace forgets
   Ye are king but o' the land!"    16

*Used by permission of Dr. Greville Macdonald and of the publishers, Kegan Paul, Trench, Trübner & Co., Ltd.

# The Earl o' Quarterdeck

And still he held to the open sea;
  And the east-wind sank behind;
And the west had a bitter word to say,
  Wi' a white-sea roarin' wind.      20


And he turned her head into the north.
  Said the king: "Gar fling him o'er."
Quo the fearless skipper: "It's a' ye're worth!'
  Ye'll ne'er see Scotland more."      24


The king crept down the cabin-stair,
  To drink the gude French wine.
And up she came, his daughter fair,
  And luikit ower the brine.      28


She turned her face to the drivin' hail,
  To the hail but and the weet;
Her snood it brak, and, as lang's hersel',
  Her hair drave out i' the sleet.      32


She turned her face frae the drivin' win'—
  "What's that ahead?" quo she.
The skipper he threw himsel' frae the win',
  And he drove the helm a-lee.      36


"Put to yer hand, my lady fair!
  Put to yer hand," quo he:
"Gin she dinna face the win' the mair,
  It's the waur for you and me."      40


For the skipper kenned that strength is strength
  Whether woman's or man's at last.

301

To the tiller the lady she laid her han',
   And the ship laid her cheek to the blast.   44

For that slender body was full o' soul,
   And the will is mair than shape;
As the skipper saw when they cleared the berg,
   And he heard her quarter scrape.   48

Quo the skipper: "Ye are a lady fair,
   And a princess grand to see;
But ye are a woman, and a man wad sail   52
   To hell in yer company."

She liftit a pale and queenly face;
   Her een flashed, and syne they swim.
"And what for no to heaven?" she says,
   And she turned awa' frae him.   56

But she took na her han' frae the good ship's helm,
   Until the day did daw;
And the skipper he spak, but what he said
   It was said atween them twa.   60

And then the good ship she lay to,
   With the land far on the lee;
And up came the king upo' the deck,
   Wi' wan face and bluidshot ee.   64

The skipper he louted to the king:
   "Gae wa', gae wa'," said the king.
Said the king, like a prince, "I was a' wrang,
   Put on this ruby ring."   68

# The Earl o' Quarterdeck

And the wind blew lowne, and the stars cam' oot,
   And the ship turned to the shore;
And, afore the sun was up again,
   They saw Scotland ance more.    72

That day the ship hung at the pier-heid,
   And the king he stept on the land.
"Skipper, kneel down," the king he said.
   "Hoo daur ye afore me stand?"    76

The skipper he louted on his knee,
   The king his blade he drew:
Said the king, "How daured ye contre me?
   I'm aboard my ain ship noo.    80

"I canna mak ye a king," said he,
   "For the Lord alone can do that;
And besides ye took it intil yer ain han'
   And crooned yersel' sae pat!    84

"But wi' what ye will I redeem my ring;
   For ance I am at your beck.
And first, as ye loutit Skipper o' Doon,
   Rise up Yerl o' Quarterdeck."    88

The skipper he rose and looked at the king
   In his een for all his croon;
Said the skipper, "Here is yer grace's ring,
   And yer daughter is my boon."    92

The reid blude sprang into the king's face,—
   A wrathful man to see:

303

"The rascal loon abuses our grace;
    Gae hang him upon yon tree."

96

But the skipper he sprang aboard his ship,
    And he drew his biting blade;
And he struck the chain that held her fast,
    But the iron was over weel made.

100

And the king he blew a whistle loud;
    And tramp, tramp, down the pier,
Cam' twenty riders on twenty steeds,
    Clankin' wi' spur and spear.

104

"He saved your life!" cried the lady fair;
    "His life ye daurna spill!"
"Will ye come atween me and my hate?"
    Quo the lady, "And that I will!"

108

And on cam' the knights wi' spur and spear,
    For they heard the iron ring.
"Gin ye care na for yer father's grace,
    Mind ye that I am the king."

112

"I kneel to my father for his grace,
    Right lowly on my knee;
But I stand and look the king in the face,
    For the skipper is king o' me."

116

She turned and she sprang upo' the deck,
    And the cable splashed in the sea.
The good ship spread her wings sae white,
    And away with the skipper goes she.

120

## The Maid

Now was not this a king's daughter,
    And a brave lady beside?
And a woman with whom a man might sail
    Into the heaven wi' pride?       124
George Macdonald.


## HEROES OF THE "TITANIC"

HONOUR the brave who sleep
    Where the lost *Titanic* lies,
The men who knew what a man must do
    When he looks Death in the eyes.     4

"Women and children first,"—
    Ah, strong and tender cry!
The sons whom women had borne and nursed,
    Remembered,—and dared to die.     8

The boats crept off in the dark:
    The great ship groaned: and then, —
O stars of the night, who saw that sight,
    Bear witness, *These were men!*     12

November 9, 1912.         Henry van Dyke.


## THE MAID

THUNDER of riotous hoofs over the
    quaking sod;
Clash of reeking squadrons, steel-capped,
    iron-shod;
The White Maid and white horse, and the flap-
    ping banner of God.

Black hearts riding for money; red hearts
    riding for fame;
The Maid who rides for France and the
    King who rides for shame—
Gentlemen, fools, and a saint riding in
    Christ's high name!        5

"Dust to dust!" it is written.  Wind-scattered
    are lance and bow.
Dust, the Cross of Saint George; dust, the
    banner of snow.
The bones of the King are crumbled,
    and rotted the shafts of the foe.

Forgotten the young knight's valor;
    forgotten, the captain's skill;    10
Forgotten, the fear and the hate and
    the mailed hands raised to kill;
Forgotten, the shields that clashed and
    the arrows that cried so shrill.

Like a story from some old book, that
    battle of long ago:
Shadows, the poor French King and the
    might of his English foe;
Shadows, the charging nobles and the
    archers kneeling a-row—    15
But a flame in my heart and my eyes,
    the Maid with her banner of snow!

*Theodore Goodridge Roberts.*

306

# THE STANDARD-BEARER

## I

"How can I tell," Sir Edward said,
  "Who has the right or the wrong o' this thing?
  Cromwell stands for the people's cause,
  Charles is crowned by the ancient laws;
English meadows are sopping red,
Englishmen striking each other dead,—
  Times are black as a raven's wing.
Out of the ruck and the mirk I see
    Only one thing!
The King has trusted his banner to me,
  And I must fight for the King."                    12

## II

Into the thick of the Edgehill fight
  Sir Edward rode with a shout; and the ring
  Of grim-faced, hard-hitting Parliament men
  Swallowed him up,—it was one against ten!
He fought for the standard with all his might,
Never again did he come to sight—
  Victor, hid by the raven's wing!
After the battle had passed we found
    Only one thing,—
The hand of Sir Edward gripped around
  The banner-staff of his King.                      22

*Henry van Dyke.*

307

# THE FORGOTTEN SOUL

'TWAS I that cried against the pane on All
    Souls' Night
    (O pulse of my heart's life, how could you
    never hear?)
You filled the room I knew with yellow
    candle-light
    And cheered the lass beside you when she
    cried in fear,             4

'Twas I that went beside you in the gray
    woodmist
    (O core of my heart's heart, how could you
    never know?)
You only frowned and shuddered as you bent
    and kissed
    The lass hard by you, handfast, as I used
    to go.             8

'Twas I that stood to greet you on the church-
    yard pave
    (O fire of my heart's grief, how could you
    never see?)
You smiled in careless dreaming as you crossed
    my grave
    And hummed a little love-song where
    they buried me!        12

                    *Margaret Widdemer.*

# THE UNKNOWN BELOVÈD*

I DREAMED I passed a doorway
    Where, for a sign of death,
White ribbons one was binding
    About a flowery wreath.      4

What drew me so I know not,
    But drawing near I said,
"Kind sir, and can you tell me
    Who is it here lies dead?"      8

Said he, "Your most belovèd
    Died here this very day,
That had known twenty Aprils
    Had she but lived till May."      12

Astonished I made answer,
    "Good sir, how say you so!
Here have I no belovèd,
    This house I do not know."      16

Quoth he, "Who from the world's end
    Was destined unto thee
Here lies, thy true belovèd
    Whom thou shalt never see."      20

---

*From the author's "Dust and Light," Scribner, 1919.

I dreamed I passed a doorway
  Where, for a sign of death,
White ribbons one was binding
  About a flowery wreath.                    24
                              *John Hall Wheelock.*


## BALLAD OF THREE

Upon the river's brink she stands
  And tastes the dawn's white breath.
She wrings her slender, silver hands,
  "God's curse on love," she saith.
"Love binds me with his cruel bands
  That break not save with death."          6


"Now Geoffrey is a huntsman bold
  And slays the mountain deer,
And Hugh plows up the fragrant mold
  And plucks the ripened ear.
In friendship would these twain grow old
  Did I not dwell anear.                    12


"Hugh brings me grapes with sunlight sweet,
  Like globes of amethyst,
While Geoffrey's fawn with snowflake feet
  Is corded to my wrist.
They mutter curses when they meet,
  Their sight dims with red mist.          18


"And it is love hath done this thing;
  Yea, Geoffrey loves my hair,

310

## Ballad of Three

And Hugh lifts up his voice to sing
   That my sad face is fair,
And love strews poison in the spring
   And fouls the pleasant air.    24

"But not for my poor loveliness
   Shall blood of brothers flow.
What is one woman, more or less?
   And what is love but woe!
I want no murderer's caress,
   So for love's sake—I go."    30

Lads, sheathe your knives, no use to fight,
   The lady you would wed
Shall sleep alone in state to-night
   With candles at her head.
Lift, friends, this figure still and white
   And bear her to her bed.    36

               *Joyce Kilmer.*

## THE RIDE TO THE LADY*

"Now since mine even is come at last,—
   For I have been the sport of steel,
And hot life ebbeth from me fast,
   And I in saddle roll and reel,—
Come bind me, bind me on my steed!
   Of fingering leech I have no need!"

---

*From "A Chant of Love for England and Other Poems," published by E. P. Dutton, New York City.

The chaplain clasped his màilèd knee.
"Nor need I more thy whine and thee!
No time is left my sins to tell;
But look ye bind me, bind me well!"                    10
They bound him strong with leathern thong,
For the ride to the lady should be long.

Day was dying; the poplars fled,
Thin as ghosts, on a sky blood-red;
Out of the sky the fierce hue fell,
And made the streams as the streams of hell.
All his thoughts as a river flowed,
Flowed aflame as fleet he rode,
Onward flowed to her abode,
Ceased at her feet, mirrored her face.                 20
(Viewless Death apace, apace,
Rode behind him in that race.)

"Face, mine own, mine alone,
Trembling lips my lips have known,
Birdlike stir of the dove-soft eyne
Under the kisses that make them mine!
Only of thee, of thee, my need!
Only to thee, to thee, I speed!"
The Cross flashed by at the highway's turn;
In a beam of the moon the Face shone stern.            30

Far behind had the fight's din died;
The shuddering stars in the welkin wide
Crowded, crowded, to see him ride.
The beating hearts of the stars aloof
Kept time to the beat of the horse's hoof.

# The Ride to the Lady

"What is the throb that thrills so sweet?
Heart of my lady, I feel it beat!"
But his own strong pulse the fainter fell,
Like the failing tongue of a hushing bell.
The flank of the great-limbed steed was wet     40
Not alone with the started sweat.

Fast, and fast, and the thick black wood
Arched its cowl like a black friar's hood;
Fast, and fast, and they plunged therein,—
But the viewless rider rode to win.
Out of the wood to the highway's light
Galloped the great-limbed steed in fright;
The mail clashed cold, and the sad owl cried,
And the weight of the dead oppressed his side.

Fast, and fast, by the road he knew;     50
And slow, and slow, the stars withdrew;
And the waiting heaven turned weirdly blue,
As a garment worn of a wizard grim.
He neighed at the gate in the morning dim.

She heard no sound before her gate,
Though very quiet was her bower.
All was as her hand had left it late:
The needle slept on the broidered vine,
Where the hammer and spikes of the passion-flower
Her fashioning did wait.     60

On the couch lay something fair,
With steadfast lips and veilèd eyne;

But the lady was not there.
On the wings of shrift and prayer,
Pure as winds that winnow snow,
Her soul had risen twelve hours ago.
The burdened steed at the barred gate stood,
No whit the nearer to his goal.
Now God's great grace assoil the soul
That went out in the wood!　　　70

*Helen Gray Cone.*


# THE BALLAD OF FATHER GILLIGAN*

THE old priest Peter Gilligan
Was weary night and day;
For half his flock were in their beds,
Or under green sods lay.　　　4

Once, while he nodded on a chair,
At the moth-hour of eve,
Another poor man sent for him,
And he began to grieve.　　　8

"I have no rest, nor joy, nor peace,
For people die and die";
And after cried he, "God forgive!
My body spake, not I!"　　　12

---

*Used by arrangement with the author's agents, A. P. Watt and Son, London, and with his American publishers, The Macmillan Company.

314

# The Ballad of Father Gilligan

He knelt, and leaning on the chair
He prayed and fell asleep;
And the moth-hour went from the fields,
And stars began to peep.                    16

They slowly into millions grew,
And leaves shook in the wind;
And God covered the world with shade,
And whispered to mankind.                    20

Upon the time of sparrow chirp
When the moths came once more,
The old priest Peter Gilligan
Stood upright on the floor.                    24

"Mavrone, mavrone! the man has died,
While I slept on the chair";
He roused his horse out of his sleep,
And rode with little care.                    28

He rode now as he never rode,
By rocky lane and fen;
The sick man's wife opened the door;
"Father! you come again!"                    32

"And is the poor man dead?" he cried.
"He died an hour ago."
The old priest Peter Gilligan
In grief swayed to and fro.                    36

"When you were gone, he turned and died
As merry as a bird."

The old priest Peter Gilligan
He knelt him at the word.                    40

"He who hath made the night of stars
For souls who tire and bleed,
Sent one of His great angels down
To help me in my need.                       44

"He who is wrapped in purple robes,
With planets in His care,
Had pity on the least of things
Asleep upon a chair."                        48

*William Butler Yeats.*